Hilang royat cerita nak timbul. . . .

South-East Asian Social Science Monographs

Malaysian Shadow Play and Music

Malaysian Shadow Play and Music

Continuity of an Oral Tradition

Patricia Matusky

KUALA LUMPUR
OXFORD UNIVERSITY PRESS
OXFORD SINGAPORE NEW YORK
1993

Oxford University Press

Oxford New York Toronto
Delhi Bombay Calcutta Madras Karachi
Kuala Lumpur Singapore Hong Kong Tokyo
Nairobi Dar es Salaam Cape Town
Melbourne Auckland Madrid

and associated companies in
Berlin Ibadan

Oxford is a trade mark of Oxford University Press

Published in the United States
by Oxford University Press, New York

© Oxford University Press 1993
First published 1993

British Library Cataloguing in Publication Data
Data available

Library of Congress Cataloging-in-Publication Data

Matusky, Patricia Ann.
Malaysian shadow play and music: continuity of an oral tradition/Patricia Matusky.
p. cm.—(South-East Asian social science monographs)
Based on the author's thesis (doctoral)—University of Michigan, 1980.
Includes bibliographical references and index.
ISBN 9676530484:
1. Dramatic music—Malaysia—History and criticism. 2. Wayang.
3. Music—Malaysia—History and criticism.
I. Title. II. Series.
ML 1751.M4M35 1993
782.1' 09595—dc20
93–1647
CIP MN

Typeset by Typeset Gallery Sdn. Bhd., Malaysia
Printed by Kyodo Printing Co. (S) Pte. Ltd., Singapore
Published by Oxford University Press,
19–25, Jalan Kuchai Lama, 58200 Kuala Lumpur, Malaysia

Preface

THIS work is based on the author's doctoral dissertation (1980) which focused on the relationship between musical sound and puppet movement in the Malay shadow play of the type known regionally in the Malaysian states of Kelantan and Terengganu as *wayang kulit Siam*, and in the southern provinces of Thailand sometimes as *wayang Kelantan*. With special attention to the music and puppet movement in the prologue (called the 'Dalang Muda'), the dissertation examined the correspondences of music and puppet movement which were analysed as analogous phenomena. The 'Dalang Muda' prologue was used as a point of special reference for several reasons: it encompasses all the basic dramatic techniques required for the performance of a story; it is a vehicle for teaching; it is ritual and social drama; and it is an overture with structural and thematic relationship to the main story in an evening's performance.

In the process of analysing the musical analogies in the 'Dalang Muda', the author's work also encompassed an examination of the socio-cultural background of the Malay shadow play, as well as a detailed description of its music, and the formulation of a theory for the musical system which, previously, had existed only in an oral tradition.

Singapore
January 1993   PATRICIA MATUSKY

Acknowledgements

THE author's methodology and preparation for field research on a traditional Malay musical/theatrical form was greatly influenced by Drs Judith Becker and William P. Malm of the University of Michigan. The author's study under Dr Becker, prior to fieldwork, prepared the way for residing in a rural Malay environment and for dealing with the multitude of situations confronting one engaged in doctoral music research in rural South-East Asia. It was Dr Becker's keen insight and guidance which helped to mould the first form of this work as a doctoral dissertation.

Dr William P. Malm provided the author with a first glimpse of the Malay performing arts from Kelantan and Kedah through his video recordings, made in the field in 1968. Dr Malm's research and recording included such forms as the Kelantanese *mak yong* dance-drama, the *wayang kulit Siam* and *wayang kulit Gedek* from Kelantan and Kedah, and the *main puteri* healing ceremony from Malaysia's east coast. The shadow forms, dancing figures, and musicians on the monitor of the video recorder, once back at the University of Michigan campus, provided the initial stimulus for further research which ultimately focused on the music of the shadow play tradition from Kelantan.

As the ethnomusicological data was gathered and a dissertation took shape, the guiding committee of scholars, with ethnomusicologist Dr Judith Becker as its chair, included Dr William P. Malm (ethnomusicology), Dr Amin Sweeney (Malay literature and culture), Dr A. L. Becker (Indonesian/Malay language and literature), and Dr William Gedney (Thai language and linguistics). The author is indebted to all for their constructive criticism and encouragement.

Dr Amin Sweeney's research and writing on the literature of the *wayang kulit Siam* shadow puppet theatre took place during the 1960s and early 1970s and, preceding the author's music research, it served as a kind of springboard from which the music research was made possible. Dr Sweeney's sponsorship of the author's field research, his aid while in Malaysia, and his criticism and guidance as a member of the author's doctoral committee in the production of this study are deeply appreciated. Many, many thanks are in order.

Other Malaysian sponsors in 1975–6 whose advice and help were well heeded include the late Ismail Zain (artist and former Director of Culture in the Malaysian Ministry of Culture, Youth and Sports), Dol Ramli (former Director of the Malaysian National News Agency), the faculty members at the National University of Malaysia (which provided academic affiliation), and Dr Ghulam-Sarwar Yousof at the Performing Arts Department of the Science University of Malaysia in Penang. Another colleague and consultant was Krishen Jit, a director of contemporary Malaysian theatre and a member of the history faculty in the University of Malaya. A Malaysianist, through Peace Corp affiliation, was the author's principal photographer, Mr Norman Farley. Mr Farley, a school-teacher in the Tumpat District of Kelantan, was a devotee of the *wayang kulit*, and his fine photography during performances, at special rehearsals, and during the author's private lessons provided many of the illustrations for the present study.

The organizations which made it economically feasible to carry out field research on the music of the shadow play during 1975–6 were the JDR 3rd Fund (presently the Asian Cultural Council) and the Office of Education (HEW), National Defense Foreign Language Fellowship Program of the United States government.

Finally, the most heartfelt thanks and deepest gratitude must be extended to the author's teachers in Kelantan. Their patience, kindness, and receptivity towards a foreigner were remarkable. The author studied with the shadow play troupe of Dalang Hamzah bin Awang Amat who was the last student of one of Kelantan's most eminent *dalang*, Awang Lah. Many musicians of Dalang Hamzah's troupe in the late 1970s were also students of Awang Lah, and their performances today still adhere closely to the tradition of that famous *dalang* of the early to mid-twentieth century.

Dalang Hamzah and his troupe are recognized not only locally but nationally as performers of great skill and excellence. The troupe is one of those often requested to perform for special state and festival occasions in and out of their home environment. Over the years Dalang Hamzah and his troupe have been sent abroad to Europe, the Middle East, the Soviet Union, Burma, and the USA to perform as the 'national *wayang kulit* of Malaysia', and in 1990 Dalang Hamzah's troupe performed in the Festival D'Avignon in France and then in Spain. Yet, the troupe's home base is still the Tumpat District and nearby Kota Bharu, Kelantan.

In addition to Dalang Hamzah, those musicians in his troupe who were the author's principal teachers in 1975–6 include Awang bin Salleh (*serunai* player) of Kampung Gerong, Muhammad Ali (drummer) of Kampung Mesira, and Ismail bin Samad (drummer) of Kampung Kebakat.

Dengan hormat saya mengucapkan setinggi-tinggi terima kasih kepada guru-guru Encik Hamzah, Encik Awang, Encik Muhammad Ali, dan Encik Ismail.

Contents

Figures

Map

Plates

Musical Examples

Musical Transcriptions

Appendices

Introduction

THE ancient, time-honoured art form known as *wayang kulit*, that is, 'leather puppet theatre' (also known as 'shadow puppet play'), is found in many parts of South-East Asia, including the Malay Peninsula. The dramatic repertoire and some aspects of the ritual (and 'magic') of the Malay shadow play have already been studied and published. Works by Anker Rentse, Jeanne Cuisinier, and Ghulam-Sarwar Yousof give informative accounts of many aspects of ritual and myth.[1] In addition, the writings of Amin Sweeney have provided information on the puppet construction and an authoritative examination of the dramatic repertoire.[2] The present work, an ethnomusicological study focusing on the musical sound and its role in the drama, is an attempt to enlighten our view of yet another aspect of the Malay shadow play.

Field Research

The initial research on the music of the Malay shadow play known as *wayang kulit Siam* was carried out during 1975–6, and subsequently was enriched by several years of residence and teaching in Malaysia, as well as some months of residence in the southern Thai province of Yala (where the Malay shadow play was also performed at one time). During 1975–6, when the author lived in Kelantan, a north-eastern Malaysian state bordering Thailand to the north-west and the Malaysian states of Pahang and Terengganu to the south, the shadow play was performed along the north-east coastal plain of Kelantan, with performances occasionally extending into the southern Thai provinces of Narathiwat, Pattani, and Yala where the author resided in the early 1980s. The '*wayang* season' began when the seasonal monsoon rains stopped, usually around February or March, and until about the mid-1980s performances of shadow play in the villages or kampongs dotting this coastal area were common up to the months of September or October. In the early 1990s, however, performances of the shadow play are no longer frequent (current local government policy gives no encouragement to such performances) and in some areas (especially in southern Thailand), the performance of the *wayang kulit Siam* has almost ceased.

The author's primary geographical area of research in the mid-1970s was the Tumpat District (see Map 1) which is predominantly a paddy-growing area. The Kelantan River is its south-eastern border, while the Golok River (which is also the national boundary between Thailand and Malaysia) and the South China Sea serve as its western and northern borders, respectively. The Pasir Mas District forms the south-western border. In the Tumpat District, which is enclosed by water on three sides, fishing is a standard occupation. However, this low coastal area proliferates with paddy-fields and it is wet-rice cultivation and vegetable farming which are the major occupations for most people in the region.

MAP 1
Tumpat District in Kelantan, Malaysia

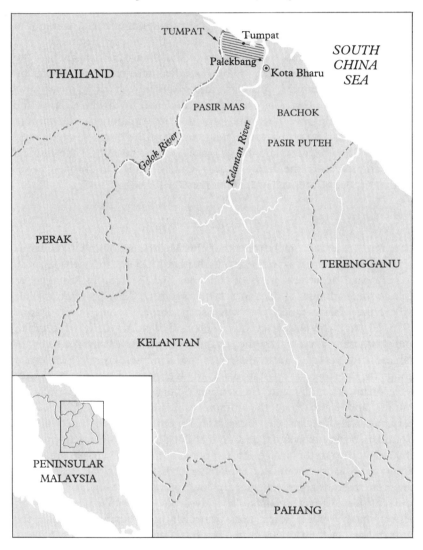

Thus, patterns of economic and cultural life revolve around the seasonal growing and harvesting cycles.

The author was able to study with a shadow play troupe which, over the past several years, has gained local as well as national recognition as one of the finest and most highly skilled troupes in Malaysia. The author's introduction to the troupe of Dalang (Puppet Master) Hamzah bin Awang Amat was made by Dr Amin Sweeney, who, at the time, was a member of the faculty of the National University of Malaysia (Universiti Kebangsaan Malaysia). The author, in effect, joined the troupe as an apprentice student of Dalang Hamzah, who lives in Kampung Gerong near the town of Palekbang. The process of formally learning *wayang kulit* happens partially within the context of performance. Consequently, in addition to daily lessons, interviews, and recordings, the author was engaged as a student performer and played various musical instruments in the orchestra as the troupe travelled from village to village, week after week. Dalang Hamzah and three additional members of his troupe became the author's principal teachers and informants. These were the shawm (*serunai*) player, Awang bin Salleh, the drum (*gendang* and *geduk*) player, Ismail bin Samad, and the all-round musician and student or deputy puppet master (*dalang muda*), Muhammad Ali. Through Dalang Hamzah and these musicians, the author was able to gain access to other troupes. Although musicians are usually associated with one specific troupe, it is also common for them to play an occasional night's show with another *dalang*. Thus, the author followed her teachers, occasionally playing with the troupe of Dalang Yusuf Hassan of Kampung Mesira, also in the Tumpat District near the town of Palekbang, and on several occasions travelling to other nearby districts to observe performances.

Transcription Techniques

The musical transcriptions of a select number of the pieces considered to be typical of Malay shadow play music and discussed in the present study are given in Appendix 4. The music was transcribed mainly from field recordings made by the author. The pieces are notated in modified staff notation in order to render the written piece as efficiently and clearly as possible. The drum rhythmic patterns for each piece, for example, are notated using standard rhythmic notation, but in addition, a clef 'signature' is used, assigning to each line of the given drum staff the name of a drum timbre in the mnemonic system used by the Malay musicians who perform the music. The modifications and other details of notation are explained in the 'Notes on the Transcriptions' at the beginning of Appendix 4. All the original field recordings made by the author in 1975–6 and in subsequent years are on permanent deposit in the Archives of Traditional Music of Indiana University (USA).

Orthography

Malay names and terms are given in the standard Malay language (Bahasa Malaysia). In some instances in which a term in the local Kelantan dialect is used, the corresponding word in standard Malay is indicated in parentheses. Proper nouns, place names, and titles preceding personal names are capitalized. Common Malay terms are printed in lower-case italics.

No written distinction is made in the Malay language between the singular and plural forms of a noun. Therefore, an effort has been made to indicate the plural attribute of the Malay nouns in the text by the addition of English numerical adjectives.

The Malay language is written in two scripts, Jawi (an Arabic-derived script) and Rumi (a Romanized script). The Malay vocabulary found in the present work is given in the Romanized script and follows the current rules for spelling in the standard Malay language.

The vowel and consonant phonemes of Bahasa Malaysia are similar to those of English. The exceptions with regard to the vocabulary of Malay words used in this book are noted below:

Malay	*International Phonetic Alphabet*
a	a
e	ɔ
é	e
i	i
u	u
au	au
ai	ai
c	tʃ
final k	ʔ (glottal stop)

1. Anker Rentse, 'The Kelantan Shadow-Play (Wayang Kulit)', *Journal of the Malayan Branch of the Royal Asiatic Society*, XIV, 3 (December 1936): 284–301; Jeanne Cuisinier, *Le Théâtre d'ombres à Kelantan*, 3rd edn., Paris: Gallimard, 1957; Ghulam-Sarwar Yousof, 'Feasting of the Spirits: The Berjamu Ritual Performance in the Kelantanese *Wayang Siam* Shadow Play', *Kajian Malaysia*, 1, 1 (June 1983): 95–115 and 'Ramayana Branch Stories in the *Wayang Siam* Shadow Play of Malaysia', in K. R. Srinivasa Iyengar (ed.), *Asian Variations in Ramayana*, New Delhi: Sahitya Akademi, 1983, pp. 296–323.

2. Amin Sweeney, *Malay Shadow Puppets*, London: The Trustees of the British Museum, 1972 and *The Ramayana and the Malay Shadow Play*, Kuala Lumpur: National University of Malaysia Press, 1972.

1
Introduction to the *Wayang Kulit* in Malaysia

Background

THE component parts of the Federation of Malaysia are the Malay Peninsula and its surrounding islands, and the two Malaysian states of Sabah and Sarawak in the northern part of Borneo. In Malaysia the shadow puppet theatre occurs only in the Malay Peninsula, most prominently in the northern states.

Socio-economic life in Peninsular Malaysia may be seen in at least two very broad styles of existence: city life with a technology-based urban environment attached to a modern and growing industrial complex (found primarily on the west coast of the Peninsula), and country life with foundations in an agriculture-based rural environment dependent primarily on rice (*padi*) cultivation and, more recently, on rubber and oil palm cultivation (found predominantly on the east coast, but to some extent in selective regions of the west coast). This dichotomy is also reflected in the social norms and cultural values found in each sector.

In Malay society, the rural kampong is where traditional values guide and determine one's mode of living and where, at least until the mid-decades of this century, traditional arts flourished. In this context, social and cultural life centres around the communal village with strong roots in Malay Islamic belief and, to some extent, in pre-Islamic belief and practice. In the late 1980s another strong tide in some regions of the rural sector is an Islamic fundamentalist fervour which adds yet another element to the contemporary outlook and values of the rural peoples. Strong adherence to *adat* (customary Malay law and practice) generally governs the family unit with regard to birth, death, marriage, and other aspects of social life and behaviour. In the villages, simple wood dwellings are built on stilts, raised about 1 metre above ground level with several houses clustered together in a small area, often surrounded by paddy-fields. In the remote, poorer communities, travel by foot or by bicycle is still common, while in the more affluent villages motor bikes and cars are usually found. The village market-place is the centre of activity during the day. In an area in which farming is the primary occupation, one's means of livelihood establishes close ties to the market where the Malay farmer defines his role as buyer as well as seller and trader of goods. The concerns of the market and of the village at large are the farmer's personal concerns.

In contrast, the urban areas, especially those on Malaysia's west coast, offer a modern, Western-influenced lifestyle. In urban society there is still adherence to traditional mores governing social behaviour. However, *adat*, traditional norms, and traditional arts tend to become buried in layer upon layer of modern values and behaviour patterns. The urban Malay is often a professional person, a civil servant, or a businessman. His dwelling is a modern cement structure built at the ground level and often equipped with the most up-to-date electrical appliances and gadgetry. His means of transportation is usually a car or motor bike, and he lives in suburban housing complexes where fences define his territory. His own private concerns usually do not involve the urban community in whole or in part. If a traditional, communal lifestyle characterizes the kampong, then a modern, individualistic mode is prominent in the urban areas.

Within these two broad socio-economic patterns, traditional Malay theatrical arts have developed and flourished in the rural, agriculture-based areas of Peninsular Malaysia. In some rural localities, particularly in the northern states of Kedah and Kelantan, the *wayang kulit* (shadow puppet theatre or shadow play) remains as one form of entertainment. Not more than fifteen years ago, it was possible to see *wayang kulit* in certain rural areas on almost any night of the week except the eve of the Muslim sabbath. The shadow play was known and enjoyed by Malays who lived in those local areas, and both the dramatic and musical aspects of the form, existing only in an oral tradition, were passed on to the young performers. With roots in the rural villages, the tradition of shadow play was, and still is, one of the major Malay folk art forms in the states of Kelantan, Kedah, and Terengganu. The type of shadow play particularly popular and widespread in these states is known as *wayang kulit Siam* in the state of Kelantan and by the term *wayang Kelantan* in some regions outside of Kelantan, including the southern Thai states bordering northern Malaysia.

Since at least the 1970s the *wayang kulit* as a form of entertainment has been given keen competition, for even in the rural paddy-growing areas, the cinema, radio, and especially television (broadcasting from the urban areas) are increasingly prevalent and popular. By the mid-1970s in many village areas in the Kota Bharu and Tumpat districts, for example, small coffee-shops installed a television set which was prominently placed inside the shop to make viewing easily accessible to all patrons who stopped by. Most evenings saw the shop packed full of people, young and old, who watched old series of programmes from American television as well as Malaysian drama or variety shows with the then current pop singers.[1]

In addition, the 'travelling' cinemas were popular in the villages during the 1970s. A high cloth fence would be temporarily erected in a given locality of the countryside, a large screen put up, and admission charged to see Malay, Indonesian, or Hindi films. This outdoor cinema would play in one place over a period of one or two nights and then move on to another location until its planned circuit was completed. These films, which were usually well attended, offered yet another form of competition, for a *dalang* (puppeteer) knew that if a film was being shown in his local area, then attendance at the *wayang kulit* would be poor. In the 1980s and 1990s televisions are commonplace in the villages. Furthermore, in the rural areas where there are now better roads and easy modes of transportation into the towns, the preference of theatre-goers tends towards the subject-matter and medium of film (or perhaps occasionally live modern drama) rather than shadow play.

In the urbanized west coast of Malaysia, the shadow play has traditionally held little significance as a form of entertainment. Although most city dwellers know about the Malay shadow play tradition, many of them also acknowledge that they have never seen or heard a performance. Under British colonial rule, and since 1957 under Malaysian rule, there has been no attempt to provide a growing, nurturing environment throughout the country for the traditional performing arts from the rural areas.[2] Instead, other forms of popular entertainment, such as the dancehalls, the *bangsawan* (Malay opera), *boria* (popular theatre), and modern (or contemporary) dramatic productions predominated in urban Malaysia, reflecting the strong influence of external elements from non-Malay cultures, particularly those of Persian, Indian, and Western or European origin.[3] In addition, traditional drama and music have never been systematically taught in public or private schools and have not been depended upon as major forms of entertainment by the large segment of the population who are urban or suburban dwellers.

In the late 1970s, however, at least two contemporary Malaysian theatre directors took a keen interest in the shadow puppet theatre. Early in 1979, at a major drama seminar held in Kuala Lumpur, the play entitled *Tok Perak* (by the Malaysian playwright Syed Alwi) was produced.[4] An abstract version of the play was performed, in part, as if it were shadow play using a *dalang* and traditional music. The drama was acted out in mime and dance by human actors instead of flat, cowhide puppets. This event marked one of the few instances in which the use and adaptation of shadow play has been seen in a contemporary theatrical setting.

The late 1970s also saw the development of a *wayang kulit* troupe in Kuala Lumpur, the federal capital of Malaysia. The troupe, known as the Kelana–Phoenix Company, was initiated through the co-operative efforts of a noted director of modern Malaysian theatre[5] and a young Kelantanese *dalang*. The troupe of musicians and the *dalang* of the Kelana–Phoenix Company comprised mainly Kelantanese migrants who had settled in and around the suburbs of Kuala Lumpur. The younger musicians of the troupe were taught by the young *dalang* who learned his art not by serving a formal apprenticeship with a teacher, but by imitation.[6] The young *dalang*, in this case, is placed in the tradition of *dalang tiru* (*dalang* by imitation), in which there is no formal instruction from a teacher. Instead, the would-be *dalang*, if he is talented enough, picks up performance techniques by observing and copying other master puppeteers. The musical and theatrical style of the Kelana–Phoenix Company stemmed directly from the *wayang kulit Siam* type of shadow play performed in the villages of Kelantan.

Also in an urban environment, a new interest in the shadow play grew in the academic world of the Universiti Sains Malaysia (Science University of Malaysia) in Penang. By the late 1970s the programme in performing arts, providing a focus on traditional Malaysian theatre, engaged teaching faculty and students in research efforts to understand the various aspects of the shadow play, as well as other Malay theatrical forms. The academic programme utilized the knowledge and skill of a practising professional puppet master, Dalang Hamzah bin Awang Amat of Kampung Gerong, Kelantan, thereby focusing on the *wayang kulit Siam* type of shadow puppet theatre. With student and, at one time, staff *wayang kulit* groups in occasional performance on the campus, the academic community, as well as the public in and around urban Penang, had, and continues to have, some contact with the shadow play tradition.

In general, however, Peninsular Malaysia presents an environment in which a very small segment of the total population knows and experiences the *wayang kulit*. In the urbanized west coast areas, some interest in the shadow puppet theatre has been realized in professional theatrical circles, while in select rural areas of the west and east coasts of the Peninsula, traditional theatre, including the shadow play, still exists as a form of entertainment. Nevertheless, the rapid influx of urban-oriented mass media and the increasingly better means of communication between the urban and rural areas point to fast-paced changes in the traditional theatrical form in its rural setting.

Types of *Wayang Kulit*

In Malaysia four main types of shadow play are (or have been at one time) performed in various regions of the Peninsula. These are *wayang kulit Jawa, wayang kulit Gedek, wayang kulit Melayu* (also known as *wayang Jawa*), and *wayang kulit Siam*.[7]

Wayang Kulit Jawa

The *wayang kulit Jawa* is basically the Javanese *wayang kulit purwa* and is performed by peoples of Javanese ancestry in the southern Malaysian states of Johor and Selangor. Performed in the Malay language along with passages in old Javanese, this type of shadow play retains the characteristics of the parent form, the Javanese *wayang kulit purwa*, including the use of the *Mahabharata* characters and stories. The finely carved and gilded puppet characters are made from leather in shapes, sizes, and colours which are distinctly Javanese in design.[8]

The gamelan of Central Java, which traditionally accompanies the *wayang kulit purwa*, consists of a large number of hanging bronze knobbed gongs (the *gong agung*, *suwukan*, and *kempul*), as well as several pot-shaped knobbed gongs (the *kenong*, *ketuk*, and *bonang*) in various-sized sets placed horizontally in wooden racks. These hanging and pot-shaped gongs have a time-marking function in the music, ultimately denoting specific musical forms such as those called *sampak*, *srepegan*, and *ayak-ayak*, the three main musical forms used to accompany the Javanese *wayang kulit*. The bronze-keyed metallophone instruments of the gamelan, such as the *sarun*, *demung*, *slenthem*, and *gender*, and the wooden xylophone called *gambang* are also percussion instruments, and provide both the basic and ornamented melodies in gamelan shadow play music.[9]

Wayang Kulit Gedek

Wayang kulit Gedek is the Malay term for the shadow puppet theatre of southern Thailand which is known as *nang talung* among the Thai peoples. This shadow puppet theatre using small leather puppets supposedly originated in the southern Thai town called Pattalung, hence the name *nang* (theatre) *talung* (an abbreviated form of the name Pattalung). Performances of this type of shadow puppet theatre can be found not only in southern Thailand, but also in the northern Malaysian states of Kedah and Kelantan, where it is performed in the Thai language or in a mixture of Thai and the local dialect of the Malay language, depending upon the particular region in which it is presented. The style of the small leather puppets and the general presentation of the *wayang kulit Gedek* take form in a distinctly southern Thai idiom, featuring the use of very thin, delicate, full- and profile-faced puppets. The small orchestra also strongly exhibits Thai features with the use of various drums, bronze gongs, cymbals, and fiddles. Formerly in Thailand the Thai shawm called the *pi* or the *pi Jawa* was included in the ensemble (a feature still present in many ensembles found in Malaysia), but in more recent times in southern Thailand there has been a preference for the Thai fiddles *saw oo* and *saw duang*.[10]

The remaining types of shadow puppet theatre, the *wayang kulit Siam* and the *wayang kulit Melayu*, are Malay types of shadow play performed by Malay peoples in the various regional dialects of the Malay language.

Wayang Kulit Melayu

The *wayang kulit Melayu*, also known as the *wayang Jawa*, is strongly influenced by the Javanese *wayang kulit purwa*. This type of shadow play once flourished under royal patronage and existed as entertainment only for aristocrats in the northern Malay sultanates of Kedah, Kelantan, and, formerly, in Pattani of present-day southern Thailand. One of the well-known Kelantanese *dalang* of the *wayang Jawa* has noted that it was, indeed, supported by the royal family up to the outbreak of World War II. Performances and court patronage ceased during the Japanese Occupation of Malaya, but performances began again, this time primarily as entertainment for the local commoners at the time of Malayan independence (*merdeka*).[11] According to Sweeney, by the 1970s there were only two *dalang* of *wayang kulit Melayu* in Kelantan, two in Kedah, and two in southern Thailand who were still able to perform.[12] In the late 1980s, however, with the loss of court patronage and the serious decline in the number of performing *dalang*, this type of shadow puppet theatre is nearly extinct.

Historically, the interest and importance of the *wayang kulit Melayu* in the Malaysian shadow play tradition lies in its ties to Javanese sources with regard to literature, theatrical conventions, and music. Sweeney, in his work on the *Ramayana* in the Malay shadow play, has noted that during the time of court patronage in the nineteenth and early twentieth centuries, many Malay *dalang* were sent to Java to learn the art of shadow puppet theatre.[13] They returned to north Malaysia with story manuscripts in hand, as well as knowledge of the theatrical conventions, orchestra, and music in the Javanese style. Back in their home settings, the Malay *dalang* continued to develop the *wayang kulit Melayu* style using a mixture of the Javanese elements they had learned in Indonesia as well as the Malay features of shadow play found in their own village environments. The stories told in the *wayang kulit Melayu*, for example, are primarily those of the Panji cycle (see Chapter 2) and the *Mahabharata*, which relates the adventures of the Pandawa clan. Some Javanese language is used in the recitation and chanting of certain passages of the text in a story; however, the predominant language used in relating the story-line, the dialogue, and the monologue is the regional Malay dialect.

Some *wayang kulit Melayu dalang* claim that there are well over 1,000 flat leather puppets in a complete set, encompassing all the characters needed to tell the Panji and Pandawa stories. The puppets used, to this day, retain a form, style, and design very similar to the Javanese leather puppets of the *wayang kulit purwa* (Plate 1). The stage itself, however, follows the traditional Malay shadow play roofed operating hut raised on stilts, with a white screen stretched over a frame to partition off the unwalled side of the hut for viewing by the audience. Like the Malay *wayang kulit Siam* folk village form of shadow puppet theatre, the *wayang kulit Melayu* orchestra players sit inside the hut behind the *dalang*. While the manipulation of the leather puppets is similar in both types of Malay shadow play, the pace of the puppet movements as well as the pace at which the story progresses is much slower in the *wayang kulit Melayu* type when compared to the fast-paced, village folk style of the *wayang kulit Siam*.

An important feature of the performance structure in the *wayang kulit Melayu* is the ritual opening of prayers and food offerings presented to the spirit world. Following the customary practice of the Malay *dalang*, the shadow play begins with incantations and prayers asking for safety and help in avoiding danger. The official *pembukaan* ('opening of the stage', similar to the *buka panggung* of the *wayang kulit Siam*) is carried out by the *dalang* who sits on the stage in front of the screen and lamp reciting charms and prayers with a tray of special food offerings.

Just as some of the theatrical conventions of the *wayang kulit Melayu* exhibit a mixture of Javanese and Malay elements, the music and orchestra, too, are a blend of traits from the two different sectors of the Malay world. In its use of many knobbed gongs, the *wayang kulit Melayu* orchestra shows some strong influence from the Javanese gamelan, the ensemble which has accompanied the *wayang kulit purwa* from ancient times. For example, in imitation of the extraordinary use of the bronze knobbed gongs in the Javanese ensemble, the *wayang kulit Melayu* orchestra features two large hanging knobbed gongs called *tetawak* or *tawak* (Plate 42), one medium-sized pot-shaped knobbed gong called *mong*,[14] a set of six small knobbed gongs in a rack called *canang* (Plates 2 and 43), and one pair of hand cymbals referred to as *kesi* (Plates 44–46). All the bronze knobbed gongs and cymbals serve as time markers in the music. In addition, the drum rhythmic patterns of the musical pieces are played on two double-headed barrel drums, the *gendang* (appearing in large and small sizes, and shown in Plate 3), while the only non-percussion instrument is the two-stringed Malay *rebab* (Plate 4), which provides melody often heard in heterophonic style along with the *dalang*'s sung part. The *tawak, canang, kesi,* and *gendang* are identical to those instruments found in the Malay *wayang kulit Siam* folk orchestra, although the number of *canang* used in the *wayang kulit Melayu* ensemble is greater.

The *rebab* of the *wayang kulit Melayu* orchestra presents an interesting example of the fusion of the Javanese and Malay styles in a musical instrument. In this case, the overall length of the instrument and the use of only two strings (tuned a fifth apart) follows the Javanese practice; the Malay *rebab* is taller in height and uses three strings (tuned a fifth and a fourth apart). In addition, the shape and thickness of the body and neck, as well as the exterior decorations on the body of the instrument, distinctly follow the design of the *rebab* played by the Malays in Peninsular Malaysia (Plate 5). In its physical construction, the largeness and thickness of the body and neck of the Malay *rebab* bring it into stark contrast with the small-bodied, thin (and fragile) appearance of the Javanese model.

Although this form of shadow puppet theatre was performed in the past exclusively for the nobility, court patronage has ceased and the form is nearly extinct today.

Wayang Kulit Siam

In contrast, the type of shadow puppet theatre known as *wayang kulit Siam* is a product of the Malay villages and is the pre-eminent form of shadow puppet theatre in Peninsular Malaysia. In the states of Kedah and Kelantan, the form is still performed, although a steady decline in the number of practising *dalang* and musicians has been evident over the past several years.[15] *Wayang kulit Siam,* however, remains the most widely performed and most popular type of *wayang kulit* in Malaysia. Its distribution and popularity extend to the states of Kelantan, Terengganu, Kedah, and at one time Perak and Pahang.[16] In addition, it is performed by Malay-speaking peoples of the south-eastern Thai provinces, namely Yala, Pattani, and Narathiwat. Interestingly, the name by which one refers to the *wayang kulit Siam* changes from place to place, reflecting a strong sense of regionalism in the tradition. The Kelantanese, for example, call their type of shadow play *wayang kulit Siam*, while in the southern Thai states the Kelantan type is sometimes referred to as *wayang Kelantan* or *wayang Siam Kelantan*. In addition, the *wayang kulit Siam* was performed by Kelantanese migrants in the state of Pahang in the late 1970s and, at that time, was billed as *wayang Pahang*.[17] Although certain aspects of performance technique, language, dramatic repertoire, puppet design, and music are common to the *wayang kulit Siam* performed in these areas, regional differences exist, and it is the various regional styles which comprise what Sweeney has called a 'complex' of *wayang kulit Siam* types.[18] The stylistic differences seem to be particularly evident with regard to language, dramatic repertoire, orchestration, and music. There are no extensive comparative studies of the regional similarities and differences in this type of shadow play; however, it is still possible to note that a basic *wayang kulit Siam* style is identifiable in any given location. The idea of regionalism in shadow play and other types of theatre is still very strong throughout Malaysia, and specific regional subtypes or styles are identified and acknowledged by the people who perform them.

From a musical point of view, in Kelantan alone at least two or three styles were distinguishable by the late 1970s, and in the districts of Tumpat, Kota Bharu, and Bachok, for example, certain differences in musical style were acknowledged and performed by the *dalang* and musicians in those areas. The number of drums or gongs used from one ensemble to another across districts varied, and occasionally a *dalang* in one location used musical pieces not commonly known to a *dalang* from another district. Some puppeteers to the east of Kota Bharu, for example, frequently used a musical piece entitled 'Seri Rama Bersiram' (the bathing scene for Seri Rama) and another known as 'Hanuman' (for the appearance of the character Hanuman). While these pieces were known and popular in the eastern districts of Kelantan, they were not familiarly used by the *dalang* from the western districts of the state. Certain *dalang*, too, might change or modernize the pieces, punctuating the music with only one hanging gong much in the style of popular social dance music known as *joget*. Siamese, Hindi, or popular Malay tunes may be played on traditional instruments with drum and gong accompaniment, and the extent to which these modern elements are used depends on the taste and inclination of the *dalang* in each specific district or region.

This work focuses on the music of the *wayang kulit Siam* as performed in the Tumpat District to the north-west of Kota Bharu, the state capital. The musical and theatrical style discussed here is acknowledged by the *dalang* and musicians in the region to be a very old style which can be traced back to Tuk Dalang Awang Lah (*c.*1898–1973), who was recognized as one of the most skilled and popular *dalang* in the Tumpat District during his time.

The shadow puppet play in Kelantan is performed primarily as a form of entertainment in the towns and villages, and for many people it is an evening's diversion from the routine of daily life. In the past the regular *wayang* season began in February or March when the monsoon rains stopped, and continued until September or October. During the season, a *wayang kulit* performance was held on any night of the week except Thursday, the eve of the Muslim sabbath. (In the 1990s there is no longer a specific *wayang* season, and the frequency of performances is steadily decreasing in the villages.) In the past it was usual for an individual or a number of people in a given village to erect a hut-like stage on which the shadow play is performed and invite a *dalang* to perform for a specific number of nights. The *dalang* himself would then obtain a performing licence from the local police authorities for the performances on specific dates and in the given location. An admission fee would be collected from the audience, and a fee paid to the *dalang* and his troupe for each night's performance.[19]

Occasionally the *wayang kulit* is staged in the context of an important ceremony known as the *berjamu* (feasting of the spirits). This high ritual event in the *wayang* world is performed only for a special occasion such as a wedding celebration, a circumcision, the demolition of an old house, the initiation of a new *panggung*, or a release from a vow. The three basic types of *berjamu* performances are known as the *pelimau* (the ritual bathing of pupils), the *pelepas niat* (release from a vow), and the *menyemah* (propitiation of spirits, for the adjustment of 'winds' or emotions).[20] When a new *wayang kulit panggung* was erected several years ago on the grounds of the Kompleks Budaya Negara (National Culture Complex) in Kuala Lumpur, the official opening and initiation of the *panggung* took place with a *menyemah* ritual performed by Dalang Hamzah bin Awang Amat himself. A *berjamu* is always a very costly event in terms of the preparation of foods and other material items and facilities, as well as the emotional and spiritual effort on the part of the *dalang* and other participants. Consequently, it is rarely performed.

1. The most popular of the American programmes during 1976–8 included such shows as 'Combat', 'Petticoat Junction', 'The Waltons', and various cowboy-and-Indian shows. The programmes were usually broadcast with Malay subtitles.

2. The performing arts in general have been seriously neglected at both primary and secondary school levels in the public education system. The federal government agencies such as the Ministry of Culture and Tourism (formerly Culture, Youth and Sports and now known as Culture, Arts and Tourism) have attempted to establish or to aid small groups of individuals interested in the traditional performing arts, but these efforts have occurred on a very small scale and have reached very few people.

3. See Tan Sooi Beng, *Bangsawan: A Social and Stylistic History of Popular Malay Opera*, Singapore: Oxford University Press, 1992, on the *bangsawan*; Rahmah Bujang, *Boria: A Form of Malay Theatre*, Singapore: Institute of Southeast Asian Studies, 1987 and 'The Boria: A Study of a Malay Theatre in Its Socio-Cultural Context', Ph.D. thesis, University of Hull, 1977, on the *boria*; and Wan Abdul Kadir, *Budaya Popular dalam Masyarakat Melayu Bandaran*, Kuala Lumpur: Dewan Bahasa dan Pustaka, 1988, on the development of the dancehalls and other forms of entertainment on radio, television, and the cinema in Malaysian popular culture.

4. The production on 12 April 1979 was directed by Krishen Jit as part of the 'Seminar Drama Melayu—25 Tahun', a seminar held to commemorate the twenty-fifth year of contemporary Malaysian drama. The seminar was jointly sponsored by the Malay Studies Department of the University of Malaya and by the Cultural Office of the Federal Territory (Kuala Lumpur).

5. Chin San Sooi, a director of theatre for many years, worked on a modern drama based on the *Ramayana* story and engaged the help of a then young *dalang*, Abdullah Mutalib Husain, to incorporate elements of the shadow play into his production. It was in this and subsequent associations with the *dalang* that Chin San Sooi formed the Kelana–Phoenix *wayang kulit* troupe. In 1977 a *wayang kulit* stage was built in Kampung Pasir Lama near Kuala Lumpur where the troupe performed almost every night for some two years. By the early 1980s the Kelana–Phoenix had lost its home in Kampung Pasir Lama; however, it continued to play in the city's shopping complexes and at the night market (*pasar malam*) in Kuala Lumpur for a short time before it disbanded.

6. Kijang Puteh, 'Talib the Boy Dalang', in *The Straits Times Annual*, 1967, pp. 62–3. The young *dalang*, Abdullah Mutalib Husain, began to observe, imitate, and practise the art of the puppet master of *wayang kulit* at the age of seven in his home village near Kota Bharu, Kelantan. Eventually a job took him to Kuala Lumpur and, sometime later, an association with the theatre director Chin San Sooi saw the birth of the Kelana–Phoenix Company with Talib as its *dalang*.

7. Amin Sweeney, *The Ramayana and the Malay Shadow Play*, Kuala Lumpur: National University of Malaysia Press, 1972, p. 3.

8. See also R. L. Mellema, *Wayang Puppets Carving, Coloring, Symbolism*, translated by Mantle Hood, Amsterdam: Koninklijk Instituut voor de Tropen, 1954.

9. Some changes in the construction of some of the bronze percussion instruments of the Indonesian gamelan have occurred in Malaysia. These changes are described, with illustrations, by Mohd. Ghouse Nasaruddin, 'Muzik Ethnik Malaysia', in *Bahasa, Kesusasteraan dan Kebudayaan Melayu*, Kuala Lumpur: Kementerian Kebudayaan, Belia dan Sukan Malaysia, 1976, pp. 162–303.

10. Michael Smithies and Euayporn Kerdchauay, 'Nang Talung: The Shadow Theatre of Southern Thailand', in Mattani Rutnin (ed.), *The Siamese Theatre: Collection of Reprints from the Journal of the Siam Society*, Bangkok, 1975, p. 132.

11. Interview in 1977 with the *wayang Jawa dalang* and *bomoh diraja* (the official traditional medicine man of the royal household), Nik Abdul Rahman bin Haji Nik Din, better known as Pak Nik Man.

12. Sweeney, *The Ramayana*, p. 3.

13. Ibid., pp. 24–5.

14. Sweeney, in *The Ramayana*, notes the use of two *mong* during the time of his research in Kelantan.

15. Sweeney, in *The Ramayana* and in *Malay Shadow Puppets*, London: The Trustees of the British Museum, 1972, p. 12, notes some 300 *dalang* in Kelantan alone during the late 1960s, although the number of practising *dalang* at that time was closer to about 100. Almost ten years later in 1976 the present author noted only five *dalang* in the Tumpat District and about twenty-five in the Kota Bharu District who were active in performing *wayang kulit* during the regular season. In the 1990s the number of active *dalang* is even less.

16. Sweeney, in *The Ramayana*, notes the performance of the *wayang kulit* Siam type of shadow play in Kelantan, Kedah, Terengganu, and Perak and from at least 1976–8 it was also performed in the state of Pahang by Kelantanese migrants.

17. Sweeney, in *The Ramayana*, also notes the vast array of names in the various regions of Malaysia and South Thailand by which the *wayang kulit* Siam is known.

18. Sweeney, *The Ramayana*, p. 4.

19. Sweeney, *The Ramayana*, pp. 26–32. Sweeney gives a detailed account of the economic aspects of the *wayang kulit* as practised in Kelantan.

20. See also Sweeney, *The Ramayana*, pp. 275–9, and Ghulam-Sarwar Yousof, 'Feasting of the Spirits: The Berjamu Ritual Performance in the Kelantanese *Wayang Siam* Shadow Play', *Kajian Malaysia*, 1, 1 (June 1983): 95–115.

2
Performance Practice

Theatrical Conventions of the *Wayang Kulit*

THE basic needs and facilities of a shadow play, requiring a screen, lamp, and actors or puppets of some kind, would appear to be universal wherever the shadow play is performed. In South-East Asia alone, however, the physical shape and dimensions of the stage and screen, type of lamp, and the performing techniques vary somewhat from the mainland to the islands of the region. In Central Thailand (and formerly in Cambodia) in the mainland region of South-East Asia, for example, the *nang yai* (or *nang sbek*) feature the large non-articulated leather puppets which stand over 1 metre high and sometimes require two men to carry and dance with them behind and in front of a very large screen.[1] In contrast, the southern Thai, Malay, and Indonesian shadow play traditions feature small leather puppets, held in the hand of a single person who articulates the movable arms and other parts of the puppet. In this case, the screen may be very small (some 1 x 2 metres as in the southern Thai form) or medium to large (about 2 x 3 metres), mounted on a free-standing frame or installed on a frame which makes up one wall of a small hut-like room (as in Indonesia or Malaysia). The types of lamps differ from one region to another, as do the types of puppet movements, the design of the puppets themselves, and, to some extent, the method of presentation.[2]

In Malaysia the shadow play is performed on a stage (*panggung*), a hut-like roofed structure built about 1 metre above ground level. The *panggung* is nearly square with about 10 square metres of floor space (about 3 x 3.6 metres). It is constructed of wood or bamboo supports, with the roof and walls of thatched reeds (*atap*), wood, or zinc. Characteristic of the Malay shadow play stage is a roof which slants downward towards the back of the hut, and extending some 0.5–1 metre beyond the opposite, front side. A similarly constructed *panggung* for the shadow play is found on the islands of Lombok and Bali in Indonesia.[3] The screen (*kelir*) is positioned so that the top of it tilts slightly towards the audience which is seated on the ground during a performance (Plates 6 and 7).[4]

Two banana tree-trunks (*batang pisang*) running the full length of the screen are laid on the floor at the base of the screen and parallel to it. The handles of the puppets are placed into these *batang pisang*, thus holding the puppets in place during a performance. The *batang pisang* closest to the screen is fixed slightly higher than the inner one which allows the *dalang* to conceal his hands as well as the handles of the puppets as he performs. An area about 1 metre along the central portion of the *batang pisang* serves as the performing space where nearly all the action takes place, while the 0.5–1 metre on either side of the performing space is used to store those puppets not in immediate use. The usual practice is to store puppets of positive or good character on the right side of the *dalang*, while those of negative or evil character are kept on the left side. The upper portion of the screen is used only occasionally, and almost all activities and puppet movements occur at the centre and base of the screen.

A lamp (*pelita*) hangs at the middle of the screen at eye-level height with the *dalang*, who sits on the floor. In former times an oil wick lamp was used; however, by the 1970s a kerosene pressure lamp or an electric bulb was a common source of light, mounted on a support of wood, cardboard, or leather which directs the light towards the screen and away from the face of the *dalang* and the musicians. The *dalang* then sits inside the *panggung* facing the middle of the screen, and the musicians sit in a specific arrangement behind him (the basic arrangement inside the *panggung* is shown in Plate 8).[5] The *dalang* manipulates the puppets between the lamp and the screen, casting shadows on the screen as he relates a tale. In Malaysia the *wayang kulit Siam* is usually a three-hour performance, beginning at about nine o'clock in the evening and concluding at midnight.

The puppets of the *wayang kulit Siam* are of the small, flat leather variety and are specific in design to the Kelantan and southern Thailand regions. The puppets are made of cowhide in ornate designs, beautifully highlighted with bright colours.[6] In the 1990s only a very small number of *dalang* in Kelantan still make puppets, and of those only a few are considered highly skilled in the art. The puppets are carved in profile from cowhide (or sometimes goat hide) which has been scraped, dried, and shaved to the proper thickness. After the puppet design has been applied to the hide (by drawing directly on it or by applying a paper drawing on to it), the basic shape and interior filigree design are carved out using small chisels of various shapes and sizes.

The colour is applied to both sides of the carved cowhide usually with enamel or water-base paints (or less often with vegetable dyes). Some contemporary *dalang* also experiment with various colours of ink, applying it with large felt-tipped pens. This method of colouring, however, is considered inferior and is not used by those puppeteers who are considered to be skilled in making puppets for the shadow play. The flat puppet is held erect by means of a narrow rod of split wood which runs the full length of the body and extends some 12–15 centimetres below the feet to serve as a handle. A smaller stick of bamboo or wood is attached to one arm which is usually the only movable part of the puppet. Some select characters, such as the two major clown-servants (Pak Dogol and Wak Long), a few country bumpkin characters, and the Javanese-style demigods have two articulated arms (in the style of the Javanese flat hide puppets) as shown in Plates 9–11. In addition, the clown-servants have movable jaws (either lower jaw or both upper and lower may be articulated) as illustrated in Plate 10. The Javanese demigods, who appear only in the context of a main story-line, are carved in Javanese design and are distinctly different in style from the Malay demigods with bows and arrows (*dewa panah*) who are reserved exclusively for use in the 'Dalang Muda' prologue.

The face and body colour is prescribed for some of the major characters, although symbolism in the use of given colours is not expressed by the *dalang* who make the puppets. The hero-prince Seri Rama is always green, Laksamana is red, as is the king of the demons Rawana, and the monkey warrior Hanuman Kera Putih is usually white, or sometimes silver. Among the female characters, the face, hands, and feet of Siti Dewi often remain unpainted except for the details of eye, mouth, ear, dress, and ornaments. The colour of the dress, and ornaments on the puppets can vary greatly, although the noble characters always wear clothing in highly filigreed design which is decorated with flowers and highlighted with gold paint. The puppets, too, vary slightly in height depending upon their maker; however, all puppets in any single set are sized proportionately to other puppets in the same set.

The main puppet characters are those derived from the *Ramayana*, the root story or epic on which the *wayang kulit Siam* is historically based. These characters include the hero-prince Seri Rama, his brother Laksamana, Rama's wife Siti Dewi, Hanuman the monkey warrior, the king of the demons Rawana, as well as Sugriwa and other warriors (Plates 12–16 and 22). Probably the most important of those characters not derived from the *Ramayana* are the two major clowns of Seri Rama's court, Pak Dogol and his cohort, Wak Long (shown in Plate 9). Others include country bumpkins or *orang darat* (Plate 11), maidens or *dayang* (Plate 17), and various characters in traditional and contemporary Malay dress.

Some experimentation has also been carried out making and using characters from Islamic legends, such as the Amir Hamzah stories, while those *dalang* heavily influenced by the southern Thai shadow play make puppets in full face wearing contemporary street clothes. The traditional puppets, such as those derived from the *Ramayana* story, exhibit the ideals of refinement (*halus*) and coarseness (*kasar*) in Malay culture with regard to their physical traits, behaviour, and speech patterns. The characters Seri Rama, Laksamana, and Siti Dewi are clear examples of refinement with slender bodies, small noses and mouths, almond eyes, and highly decorated clothing (as shown in Plates 12, 13, and 16). These refined puppets have delicate voices and move in small, slow gliding steps with a subtle swaying of the body and gentle movement of the arms. In contrast, the king Rawana as well as the various warriors, the monkey Hanuman, and the ogres (*raksaksa*) exhibit unrefined characteristics such as broad, bulbous noses, big round eyes, and large mouths often with teeth showing (Plates 15 and 22). The voice quality of these characters is always loud and boisterous and their movements are generally fast, large, and often jerky in nature with large gesticulations of the single movable arm. The commoners and country bumpkins, of course, are the epitome of coarseness with round eyes and noses, pot-bellies, large behinds, and sarong-clad torsos (Plate 11). The speech patterns of these characters are usually vulgar to the extreme with comical, nasalized voices punctuated by quick, jabbing-like movements of the arms. In addition to the major categories of puppet types, including noble princes and princesses, warriors, sages, commoners, clowns, and ogres, there are also animals, demigods, and non-animate objects such as weapons, the receiving hall or *balai* (Plate 14) of the palace, and the banyan tree or *pokok beringin* (Plate 18). The *pokok beringin,* representing the tree of life, in the Malay shadow play is comparable to the mountain (*gunungan* or *kayon*) of the Javanese *wayang kulit purwa*.[7] It always appears at the beginning and end of a performance, and in the context of a given story, it may be used to indicate wind, fire, water, and other phenomena found in the natural environment. Like the Javanese *gunungan*, in the Malay tradition the banyan tree also encapsulates the essence of all things in the *wayang*, thus reflecting all phenomena and objects in the natural world. The *pokok beringin* has a basic tree (and mountain-like) shape filled with animals, birds, reptiles, flowers, and branches, all entwined to compose a filigreed whole—a unity of plant and animal, structured in mirror imagery.

The root story of the *wayang kulit Siam* is the Malay oral version of the *Ramayana* epic, which is known as the 'Cerita Maharaja Rawana' [The Tale of King Rawana]. Although rarely performed, it is usually the first story a student *dalang* learns.[8] Although the root story comprises many specific episodes (such as the example appearing in Appendix 1), the tendency in the 1990s is to perform only a highly shortened and condensed version of the complete tale.[9]

The more frequently told stories are referred to collectively as *cerita ranting* (branch stories), while the lesser known ones are called *cerita bunga* (flower stories) and *cerita daun* (leaf stories).[10] The *cerita ranting* are not a part of the main root tale, but are peripherally related to it through the use of themes, characters, or later generations of characters related to the original *Ramayana* characters. One of the popular *cerita ranting* told by the *dalang* in Kelantan in the 1970s and 1980s is entitled 'Wak Long Menjadi Raja' [Wak Long Becomes a King]. Here, the main connection of this tale to the root dramatic repertoire is the central character Wak Long, while other *Ramayana* characters may make an occasional appearance but do not feature prominently in the story.

Sweeney, in his work on the *Ramayana* in the Malay shadow play, notes that although a great number of themes are used in the *cerita ranting,* one of the major influences on these stories is the Panji tales. Many of the tales from this cycle of stories, such as 'Ken Tambuhan' [The Remarriage of Siti Dewi and Seri Rama], 'Kerak Nasi' [The Crust of Rice], and 'Kera Mas' [The Golden Monkey], have been adapted and taken into the *wayang kulit Siam* dramatic repertoire as *cerita ranting* with the change of characters' names and some minor change of detail in the general story-line.[11] Other main sources of *wayang kulit Siam* stories are traditional Malay folk-tales, and those stories derived from local and current events.[12] *Dalang* in the 1970s and 1980s and even up to the 1990s use stories incorporating current political events, particularly at local and national election times in Malaysia.

Performance: Preliminary Ceremonies

A single shadow play story usually takes four or five nights to complete. Before the *dalang* commences with the main story-line, however, it is believed that several preliminary ceremonies must be carried out for a successful performance. The first night of the show begins with two main events, the 'feasting' (*kenduri*) and the official 'opening of the stage' (*buka panggung*). When performing at a new location and on a new *panggung* prepared for the performance, some troupes arrive at the location before darkness falls. On the ground just outside the *panggung*, they set out all the musical instruments and folios containing puppets and other accessories needed for the performance. The large hanging gongs of the orchestra are temporarily suspended from a large piece of bamboo which is supported at one end on the shoulder of a musician who stands on the ground and at the other end on a beam of the floor boards which support the *panggung*. The drums, small gongs, and cymbals are set up on the ground around the hanging gongs. On cue from the *serunai* (shawm) player, the ensemble plays an abbreviated version of the musical piece or *lagu*[13] entitled 'Bertabuh' (to signal the beginning of the shadow play). This short rendition of the piece, played outside the *panggung*, is done by some *dalang* only on the first night of a series of nights during which the troupe is performing on a new or a reopened site. At the conclusion of the music, all instruments, puppets, and accessories are taken into the *panggung* and the screen is put in place. When this brief ceremony, carried out on the ground, cannot be done at the new or reopened *panggung*, it may be performed at the *dalang*'s residence before he and his musicians leave for the performance site. Although this ceremony is not considered to be an official part of the opening of the stage, it is a custom formerly followed by some *dalang* of the *wayang kulit Siam*.

By the time the screen and other stage facilities are made ready for the performance, darkness has fallen and the *dalang* begins the *kenduri*, a ceremony in which foodstuffs and prayers are offered for the purpose of purifying the area where the *wayang kulit* will be performed.[14] A tray of food offerings (*sajian*), including cooked and raw rice, egg, flour cakes, water, and a small amount of money, is prepared. No music accompanies the *kenduri* itself, but prayers are recited throughout the ceremony.[15]

The *buka panggung* proper begins as a bit of cooked rice is smeared on each of the instruments and a small amount of water is placed inside each of the large, hanging gongs. In addition, incense is burned in a small receptacle and passed among all the musical instruments and puppets. Several puppets, including the special clowns Pak Dogol and Wak Long, are bathed separately in the smoke of the burning incense and, of these, specific ones are placed on the screen. The *pokok beringin* is placed at mid-screen thus providing a barrier between the characters of good and evil demeanour who are placed to the right and left of the *dalang*, respectively. Next, the two *dewa panah* are set facing each other on either side of the *pokok beringin*. The *dewa panah* with unrefined, Rawana-like facial traits, representing the forces of evil and also referred to as the *dewa laki-laki* or male godling, is placed on the left, while the *dewa panah* with refined facial characteristics similar to Seri Rama, representing the forces of good and referred to as the *dewa perempuan* or female godling, sits on the right side. In addition, the sage (Maharisi Kala Api) is placed at the centre of the *pokok beringin* (Plate 19), in effect, serving as the mediator between the good and evil elements. As the *dalang* sits before the screen and lamp, quietly reciting his charms during the *buka panggung*, he bends low to the floor and covers himself with a shawl. At the conclusion of his barely audible recitation, he shouts out the syllable 'hei' and suddenly sits upright. At the same time he throws the shawl from his head and shoulders and scatters parched rice over the screen, the puppets, and the musicians.

The shout-cum-sudden movement is the signal to the ensemble to begin the *lagu* 'Bertabuh', this time in its full-length form. Small amounts of water and more rice are sprinkled over all the instruments and the puppets, and the *dalang* thus concludes the ceremony with the stage officially opened.

At the conclusion of the tune 'Bertabuh', the musicians play various pieces of popular music, including old Malay pop or folk tunes, to fill in the time until the prologue to the main story begins. Some *wayang kulit* troupes also play several pieces borrowed from the *mak yong* dance-drama, including the 'Bertabuh Mak Yong' (the *lagu* for signalling the beginning of the Malay dance-drama), 'Sedayung', 'Kijang Mas', and the various types of *lagu* 'Barat'. Although some of these numbers are originally vocal pieces in the *mak yong* repertoire, they are played at this point in the *wayang kulit* with only the *serunai* carrying the melody.

The official opening of the stage and the musical interlude is followed by a prologue called the 'Dalang Muda'. After the prologue, the orchestra plays a specific piece for changing the *dalang* (*lagu* 'Bertukar Dalang') at which time the Tuk Dalang (master puppeteer) takes the stage and performs the main story for the evening. The following night the 'Dalang Muda' prologue is performed again, and a continuation of the story follows. The *buka panggung* is dispensed with since the stage has already been officially opened on the first night. On each of the subsequent four or five nights, the 'Dalang Muda' prologue is repeated and the continuation of the tale takes place, until the entire story has been related.

The 'Dalang Muda' Prologue

Every performance of the *wayang kulit Siam* includes a prologue, a ritual opening which takes slightly less than one hour to perform. The prologue is known as 'Tuk Dalang Muda' (or simply, 'Dalang Muda'), that is, 'the part performed by the student or deputy puppeteer'. It is the same in dramatic and musical content each time it is performed. It is the unchanging part of the *wayang* and, in a sense, it is a microcosmic view of the *wayang kulit*, for it involves all the techniques one needs to know in order to perform the shadow play. These techniques include spoken dialogue and narration, voice changes, singing, instrumental music, cueing devices, and puppet manipulation of all types.

In the context of the Malay *wayang kulit* tradition, the prologue serves several important functions. Didactic in nature, the 'Dalang Muda' is a vehicle by which the young student *dalang* learns the art of *wayang kulit*. It is, in fact, the first part a young student *dalang* learns from his teacher. As it is performed each night by the student (before the main story begins), it is an opportunity for him to exhibit all the skills of *wayang* which he has mastered at a given time. Even though he may not be skilled in all aspects of '*dalang*ship', the student uses the prologue to display what he already knows, as well as to improve his skill. In effect, learning to master the 'Dalang Muda' is the traditional process in which the educational experience of a student *dalang* is manifest. By the time the student begins to perform the prologue, he must already know the orchestral parts for most of the instrumental and vocal pieces of the repertoire, and he must also have a firm grasp of the dramatic repertoire. As the learning process continues, he is taught fixed spoken narration, dialogue, and stereotyped voice qualities for specific character-types, and he must also begin to sing specific pieces which appear in the second part of the prologue.

In addition, the student begins to learn the intricate patterns of puppet manipulation and the ways in which the movement of the puppets coincides and synchronizes with the music. Puppet manipulation includes specific movements for battle, walking or parading by characters of all types, the entrance and exit of characters and props, flying and descent from the heavens, the swaying or waving of the *pokok beringin*, and the posture of obeisance. In order to execute these and other highly stylized movements, specific music with its own distinctive tempo, rhythmic patterns, and musical structure are necessary. Thus, the student *dalang* must have at his command a thorough knowledge of all the basic musical pieces in the *wayang kulit Siam* repertoire.[16] Also, the deputy or student puppeteer must know how to cue the musical ensemble to begin and end a piece of music.

Most of the audience arrive at the *panggung* during the course of the performance of the 'Dalang Muda'. The music and activity of the show itself can be heard at a great distance in a given locality. Thus, the prologue also serves as an announcement or signal that the *wayang* is taking place and that the main story will begin in due time.

Musically, the prologue is an overture in the fullest sense with structural and thematic relationship to the music which accompanies the main story. The musical pieces used are both vocal and purely instrumental pieces, some of which are played (in similar rendition) from time to time during the main story itself. The musical pieces in the 'Dalang Muda' represent, from a structural point of view, every type of musical form which exists in the entire musical repertoire of the *wayang kulit Siam*. All other musical pieces found outside the 'Dalang Muda' are based on musical forms found within it.

The prologue also serves as a means to heighten and give emphasis to that which immediately follows, that is, to the main story for the evening and to the performance by the master *dalang* himself. Regular viewers of *wayang kulit* have seen the prologue as many times as they have attended a *wayang* performance and they know the dramatic and musical events which take place, that is, they know what to expect. The exact topic of the main story for the evening, however, is not known until the master *dalang* begins. Thus, the prologue, with its unchanging content and form, serves to heighten the anticipated experience of the *wayang*-goer for the main story of the evening. Also, the physical change from student (or deputy) to master *dalang* at the end of the prologue lends dramatic poignancy to the performance, and this change of puppeteers is enhanced and signified by the rendition of a special musical piece.

As ritual, the 'Dalang Muda' serves a propitiatory function as one part of a larger complex of ceremonies designed to appease certain spirits which, in past centuries, were important in traditional Kelantanese belief. Tradition dictates that the spirits important to the *wayang* world have to be appeased to eliminate any possible threat to the performance of a shadow play. The first ceremony which begins the propitiation is the *kenduri*, and this is followed by the *buka panggung* ceremony. The propitiatory rites continue in the first part of the 'Dalang Muda' prologue in which a sage (named Maharisi Kala Api) recites incantations and two *dewa panah* descend to the stage to battle. In contrast, the second part of the 'Dalang Muda' prologue features the main heroes of the *Ramayana* who are introduced and who pay homage to their leader, Seri Rama.[17]

The first main part of the prologue concerning the sage and demigods comprises four sections, each of which is defined and delineated by a specific action and musical piece as follows: (1) 'Maharisi' (*lagu* for the appearance of the sage), (2) 'Dewa Panah Turun' (*lagu* for the demigods with bows and arrows to descend from the heavens), (3) 'Dewa Panah Perang' (*lagu* for the demigods with bows and arrows to battle), and (4) 'Dewa Panah Berjalan' (*lagu* for the demigods with bows and arrows to walk together and ascend back to the heavens).

In the first section or *lagu* of the prologue, the sage, Maharisi Kala Api, is established as a dramatically and symbolically important figure, for it is he who recites the incantations to invite the two *dewa panah* to descend from the heavens to battle. The battle occurs to purify the stage and environs from any bad or otherwise undesirable elements and, thus, ensure a good performance. In this ritual the *dalang* as the prime actor communicates with other-worldly beings to ensure safety, peace, and harmony for a good performance.[18] In the context of the prologue to a shadow play, the sage, Maharisi, may be seen as an extension of the *dalang* whose mental journey to contact other-worldly beings is realized through the Maharisi's incantations. The meanings of many of the words chanted by the Maharisi are unknown, and some words or syllables in the incantation vary from one *dalang* to another. However, one possible invocation is recited as follows:

Om, om, sisi praksi pertidek yaul maupul maupul
aul maupul maupul kenong siam,
kautor dokmar ton tian bochar tuan ni wal wei

(*gertak perkakas*, a momentary beating on the musical instruments)

Om, om perbu perban platek platan dokmar dokcho
kechaipitan pakian badi me om som se.[19]

Through the invocation, then, contact is made with the spirit world, and the descent of the two *dewa panah* is followed by the presentation of these demigods before the Maharisi Kala Api. The two demigods battle fiercely, both the appearance of the demigods and their battle symbolizing the conflict and contrast of many elements in the *wayang kulit*. One aspect of contrast is the difference in the condition or state of 'refinement' and 'coarseness' which is physically represented in the make-up of the demigods themselves. The *dewa panah* on the right side of the *dalang* is characterized by refined physical features such as a small pointed nose and mouth, a smooth line running from the forehead to the nose, and an almond-shaped eye with thin brow. As noted above, this demigod is referred to as the *dewa perempuan*. In contrast, the *dewa panah* on the *dalang*'s left—the *dewa laki-laki*—has coarse features, including large round eyes, a bulbous nose, a large mouth with visible teeth, and an angular jaw line. The refined demigod carries facial features similar to Seri Rama, the hero-prince of the *Ramayana*, the root story of the dramatic repertoire for the *wayang kulit Siam*. The unrefined demigod has facial features like Rawana, Seri Rama's main adversary in the tale. In this context, then, the battle of the two demigods is symbolic of the first confrontation and conflict between the two principal characters in the shadow play. These events at the beginning of the prologue are given added dramatic effect by the generous use of space with large movements and much action in the upper regions of the screen (Plates 20–21), and by the dynamic use of the *geduk* (a short, double-headed barrel drum) which always signifies violent or strong action. Immediately after the battle, the two demigods parade across the screen together. If the battle (Plate 21) may be seen as symbolic of the contrast and confrontation of 'good and evil' as well as 'refined and coarse' elements, then the parading of the two demigods may be seen as conciliation and resolution. With the *panggung* appropriately cleansed and prepared for the performance of the main story, the two *dewa panah* ultimately ascend back to the heavens to their other-worldly origins.

The second main part of the prologue concerning the hero-prince Seri Rama consists of five sections. It appropriately enough opens with (1) the *lagu* 'Seri Rama Keluar' (the music used to signal the appearance of Seri Rama),[20] followed in sequence by (2) 'Hulubalang Seri Rama' (used for the parading of Seri Rama's warriors), (3) 'Menyembah' (used for paying homage to Seri Rama), (4) 'Berkhabar' (used for giving news of, to, and by Seri Rama), and (5) 'Seri Rama Masuk Istana' (used to accompany Seri Rama entering the palace).[21]

In contrast to the first half of the prologue which serves a propitiatory role, the second half of the prologue is a drama in which views of social conduct in Malay society are stated (and reiterated) each time the prologue is performed. The introduction of the *Ramayana* characters functions as the social drama in which proper human conduct of the past and present is told.

Codes of conduct are partially related in the language of the *wayang kulit*. The use of certain personal terms of address indicates the specific place or status in society for both the addresser and addressee, and also denotes the qualities of modesty and humility which are considered to be proper modes of social conduct. For example, the term *patik* (slave, I, me) is always used when addressing a ruler, while the term *hamba* (slave, I, me, we, us)—used to humble oneself—denotes an absence of pride and assertiveness on the part of the addresser. Although *hamba* is no longer used as a personal term of address in the standard Malay language, it is still common in rural Kelantan society and in the *wayang kulit*. These terms, as well as *Tuanku* (Your Highness), *kanda* (elder friend of a royal child), and *aku* (I, me, used in intimate circles), occur in the spoken and sung texts of the shadow play,[22] and they serve to reiterate the proper forms of communication, in both historical and contemporary contexts, in Malay society.

Specific dramatic actions, too, serve to inform the viewer of his proper role and mode of behaviour. Although the second part of the prologue consists of five distinct sections (or musical/dramatic pieces), the social drama takes form as four basic events. These events are the appearance of a noble character (Seri Rama), the act of obeisance, the event of giving news by a ruler, and, finally, the formality of parting company among characters of specific social status. Although certain portions of the social drama retain actions and characteristics peculiar to a former feudal society, others such as the act of obeisance and the formality of parting company remain relevant to contemporary social practice.

The appearance of noble characters occurs for the first time in the drama during the scene 'Seri Rama Keluar'. In this scene the importance of the characters Seri Rama and Laksamana is stressed by the singing of a special text known as the *bilangan* (also called the *ucap*). This text, in the form of rhythmic prose, formally describes and comments on the princely characters[23] and may be seen as a kind of ceremonial introduction which precedes the initial appearance of the characters on the screen. As the ornamented vocal line of sung text begins, one famous *dalang*'s rendition of the *bilangan* for Seri Rama is as follows:

Hilang royat cerita nak timbul,
ah, timbul nak royat sebuah negeri seorang raja,
raja bernama Seri Maharaja Seri Rama,
adik bernama raja muda Laksamana,
silakan adik keluar dalam istana adiklah, ah. . . .[24]

> A story was told about a country and a ruler,
> the ruler was King Rama,
> his brother was the young prince Laksamana,
> and they appeared before the palace. . . .

The introduction of the king is followed by the first appearance of the king's chief minister and warriors. After the warriors have appeared and gathered before the ruler's palace with the piece entitled 'Hulubalang Seri Rama', the scene and musical piece 'Menyembah', which tells of paying homage to the ruler as an appropriate act, follows. The first act is to assemble at the receiving hall of the palace and execute the gesture of homage or obeisance (*sembah*) before the king. The *dalang* conveys all information about these events through sung text. Each of the sung lines is followed, in turn, by the entrance of the particular warrior who does obeisance before Seri Rama and Laksamana. The social drama in the scene 'Menyembah' points to a historical past and relates to the viewer the proper code of conduct which was important at one time in Kelantanese history. The King of Malaysia, as a figurehead, is still given due respect by the gesture of obeisance.

The social drama continues to unfold as information about the state of the land is exchanged between Seri Rama and his warriors. This formality occurs in the scene and *lagu* 'Berkhabar' (Plate 23).

Finally, Seri Rama and Laksamana enter the palace and the warriors depart in the scene called 'Seri Rama Masuk Istana' (Seri Rama enters the palace). The formal announcement to part company is made in the introductory text sung by the *dalang*, reiterating the appropriate social gestures to take one's leave. The formal announcement to part company is still maintained as a proper social gesture in both rural and urban Malay society. As each of the events of the second part of the 'Dalang Muda' unfolds, certain aspects of the viewer's historical and contemporary world are made apparent. The proper forms of communication and specific ceremonies which are appropriate within given social parameters are told in the shadow play through the dramatic action of the introduction of the *Ramayana* characters.

The Musical Repertoire

In the prologue and in the main story as well, drama occurs essentially through the elements of dialogue, narration, puppet movement, and musical accompaniment. These are the interrelated fabric of the *wayang kulit*, and by hearing or seeing even one of these elements in a segment of a scene, the viewer will learn, at least in part, what the given segment of the scene is about. The viewer who hears the musical piece 'Perang' [Battle], for example, immediately knows that a battle or some kind of strong or violent action is taking place, and that a conflict is happening in the drama. Another musical piece, 'Hulubalang' [Warriors], used to accompany the appearance and parading of warriors on the screen, will tell the viewer that these characters are now involved in the drama. Thus, musical pieces define particular stereotyped actions, often by specific character types, and delineate the action in the context of scenes or segments of scenes. In effect, a given *lagu* or a number of *lagu* may define an entire scene which may include subscenes, for example, a battle scene, a letter-reading scene, a scene for paying homage, and a scene for the parading of the warriors.

To understand the role played by the music in a performance of a story, it is important to know when specific pieces and specific musical forms occur in the drama. Some musical pieces accompany the appearance and movement of particular characters or character-types, while other pieces are meant to evoke a mood or depict a certain activity. The various *lagu* to accompany the movement of walking, for example, are numerous and accompany the stereotyped walking movement for specifically named puppets (Seri Rama, Pak Dogol, and the Maharisi), as well as for character-types including demigods (*dewa*), demigods with bows and arrows (*dewa panah*), spirit-fairies (*pari*), warriors (*hulubalang*), animals (*binatang*), country bumpkins (*orang darat*), and maidens (*dayang*).

In contrast, several different kinds of action may be depicted in a single piece of music. For example, the piece commonly known as 'Menghendap' (*lagu* for crouching in ambush) may also be used for the related actions of averting danger (in which case it is known as *lagu* 'Menghindar') or hunting (*lagu* 'Memburu'). The piece usually known as 'Tidur' (*lagu* for sleeping) encompasses an even wider range of activities, including the events of lulling (*lagu* 'Mengulit'), bathing (*lagu* 'Mandi'), drinking (*lagu* 'Minum'), picking flowers (*lagu* 'Memetik Bunga'), and letter reading (*lagu* 'Baca Surat'). The *dalang* draws upon such pieces from the musical repertoire as they are appropriate in the drama (see Appendix 2).

As an evening's tale is told, the music the orchestra plays has an important role, for puppet movement never occurs without a musical piece or some other sound from the orchestra. One frequently heard sound which is not considered to be a musical piece is a short, quick ad lib beating on the drums and gongs called the *gertak perkakas*. It occurs when very brief puppet movement is executed, and may or may not be cued by the *dalang*. The musicians simply follow the action on the screen. It is used, for example, when a puppet is quickly turned to face another character in the course of ongoing dialogue, or when a very fast exit or entrance of a puppet is necessary. The brief beating on the instruments is also heard to underline certain dialogue, to add emphasis to what is said at a given point in the drama, to underline the punch line of a joke, to conceal a verbal mistake, and to give the *dalang* a moment to catch his breath in the course of the dialogue.[25]

In contrast to the *gertak perkakas*, specific *lagu* accompany the prolonged puppet movement on the screen, or the conveyance of particular information or a special mood in the form of a sung piece. At these times in the drama the *dalang* draws on a specific *lagu* from the musical repertoire. The musical pieces on which the *dalang* relies to accompany the puppet movement encompass the musical elements of formal structure, drum rhythmic patterns, and in some instances specific melodies.

1. See also the articles on the shadow theatre of Cambodia in Mohd. Taib Osman (ed.), *Traditional Drama and Music of Southeast Asia*, Kuala Lumpur: Dewan Bahasa dan Pustaka, 1974; Mattani Rutnin, 'Nang Yai: The Thai Classical Shadow Play and the Wat Kanon Troupe of Rajburi', *East Asian Cultural Studies*, 15 (March 1976): 53–9; Michael Smithies, 'The Giant Shadow Play of Thailand', *Orientations*, 4, 8 (August 1973): 47–50, and 'Thai Shadow Play Figures', *Arts of Asia*, 3, 5 (September–October 1973): 38–42.

2. The small articulated shadow puppets and their method of presentation are noted in Michael Smithies and Eauyporn Kerdchauay, 'Nang Talung: The Shadow Theatre of Southern Thailand', in Mattani Rutnin (ed.), *The Siamese Theatre: Collection of Reprints from the Journal of the Siam Society*, Bangkok, 1975; S. D. Humardani, 'The Wayang Kulit Drama: Its Traditional Stage Performance in Indonesia', in Mohd. Taib Osman (ed.), *Traditional Drama and Music in Southeast Asia*, Kuala Lumpur: Dewan Bahasa dan Pustaka, 1974, pp. 82–5; Claire Holt, *Art in Indonesia: Continuities and Change*, Ithaca, NY: Cornell University Press, 1967.

3. As noted in H. I. R. Hinzler, *Wayang op Bali*, The Hague, 1975.

4. See also Amin Sweeney, *Malay Shadow Puppets*, London: The Trustees of the British Museum, 1972, p. 10.

5. See also Shahrum bin Yub, 'The Technical Aspects of the Kelantan Malay Shadow Play Theatre', *Federation Museums Journal*, New Series, XV (1970): 43–75.

6. For a detailed account of puppet construction, see Sweeney, *Malay Shadow Puppets*.

7. See Holt, *Art in Indonesia*, pp. 134–5.

8. Amin Sweeney, *The Ramayana and the Malay Shadow Play*, Kuala Lumpur: National University of Malaysia Press, 1972. See Sweeney's work for a detailed account of the *Ramayana* epic in the *wayang kulit Siam*.

9. A synopsis of a condensed version of the *Ramayana* story, as performed by a *wayang kulit Siam dalang* in 1976, may be found in Patricia Matusky, *Music in the Malay Shadow Puppet Theater*, Vols. I–II, Ann Arbor: University Microfilms, 1980.

10. See Sweeney, *The Ramayana*, Chapter 11, which comments extensively on *cerita ranting* used in the Malay shadow play.

11. Ibid., p. 264. See also S. Robson, *Waṇbaṇ Wideya*, The Hague: Martinus Nijhoff, 1971, pp. 12–13. Robson states: '... the following outline of plot can be selected as reflecting the central elements of the Panji theme. In Java, where the story is set, there are two kingdoms, Kuripan and Daha (the various alternative names also occur), of which the former is the senior. The prince of Kuripan is betrothed to the princess of Daha but, before they can marry, a complicating factor (or combination of factors) intervenes. (For example, the princess may be lost, or be carried off, and have to be found, or a foreign king may attack and have to be defeated.) When the problems have been solved by the prince, in disguise and using an alias, then he can finally reveal himself and claim the princess. With their marriage the world returns to its former settled state. Such is the lowest common denominator of the Panji theme, although this frame can be expanded to include a great variety of episodes, elaborate descriptions and repetitions.' Holt, *Art in Indonesia*, p. 274, also states that 'the names of certain personages, of the principal kingdoms and some of the events evoke historical associations with historical East Java. It is thought that the Panji romances originated there some time in the fifteenth century. From East Java they spread to Malaya, Thailand and Cambodia. ...'

12. See also Ghulam-Sarwar Yousof, 'Ramayana Branch Stories in the *Wayang Siam* Shadow Play of Malaysia', in K. R. Srinivasa Iyengar (ed.), *Asian Variations in Ramayana*, New Delhi: Sahitya Akademi, 1983, pp. 296–323.

13. The term *lagu* may be translated as 'musical piece'. However, the variable meaning of the term in the context of the *wayang kulit* is not unlike the term *pathet* (mode) in the context of Javanese shadow play and music. In the Javanese case, the term *pathet* refers to varying musical parameters as well as sections of a drama. See A. L. Becker, 'Text-Building, Epistemology, and Aesthetics in Javanese Shadow Theatre', in A. Yengoyan and A. L. Becker (eds.), *The Imagination of Reality: Essays in Southeast Asian Coherence Systems*, Norwood, NJ: Ablex Publishing Co., 1979, pp. 220–1.

14. Anker Rentse, 'The Kelantan Shadow-Play (Wayang Kulit)', *Journal of the Malayan Branch of the Royal Asiatic Society*, XIV, 3 (December 1936): 285.

15. Ibid.

16. A list of the complete repertoire of musical pieces as performed by the various *dalang* in the Tumpat District and by many *dalang* in the Kota Bharu District of Kelantan is given in Appendix 2.

17. Sweeney, *The Ramayana*, p. 59. Events as described by Sweeney in 1972 are identical to those observed and learned by the author during her research in Kelantan in 1976. In *The Ramayana*, pp. 212 and 221, Sweeney also gives reference to the possible origins of the characters Maharisi and the *dewa panah* (which are also found in the Thai shadow play tradition).

18. In the more complex *berjamu* (feasting of the spirits) ritual, the role of the 'Dalang Muda' prologue as a propitiatory event is made even more significant, for at the mid-point of the prologue another powerful play to conciliate the spirits, called 'Tuk Peran Hutan' [The Jungle Clown], is inserted. See Sweeney, *The Ramayana*, p. 276. It is interesting to note, too, that in the *berjamu* ritual, the *dalang*'s communication with the spirit world is done directly in a state of trance.

19. See also Sweeney, *The Ramayana*, pp. 348 and 408. Sweeney includes the translation of some words of the invocation. The meaning of the entire chant, however, is unknown.

20. Also known as *lagu* 'Seri Rama dengan Gedumbak' (the musical piece for Seri Rama appearing played on the *gedumbak*).

21. Also known as *lagu* 'Berjalan' (the musical piece for walking by refined characters).

22. The translation of terms is based on Richard Winstedt, *An Unabridged Malay–English Dictionary*, 6th edn., Kuala Lumpur: Marican & Sons (Malaysia) Sdn. Bhd., 1965.

23. Sweeney, *The Ramayana*, pp. 65–72. Sweeney gives a number of *bilangan* for Seri Rama as told by different *dalang*.

24. As sung by Tuk Dalang Hamzah bin Awang Amat.

25. These uses of the *gertak perkakas* are also noted by Sweeney in *The Ramayana*.

3
The Orchestra and the Musicians

THE orchestra for the *wayang kulit* found in the northern Malaysian states is a percussion-dominated ensemble consisting of an aerophone, membranophones, and bronze idiophones. In Kelantan the instrumentation of a complete ensemble includes one quadruple-reed aerophone known as the *serunai*, three pairs of drums called *gedumbak*, *geduk*, and *gendang*, two sets of gongs called *canang* and *tetawak*, and two pairs of small hand cymbals known as *kesi*.[1]

Aerophones

The only aerophone present in the ensemble, the *serunai*, is a reed pipe and is the principal melodic instrument. It appears in two sizes, large and small, referred to as *ibu* (mother) and *anak* (child), respectively (Plate 24). The small size is usually about 40 centimetres in length and the large is at least 50 centimetres long. The size of the *serunai*, however, is not standardized and the length may vary slightly from one pair to another.

The instrument is made of a conical tube of hardwood (with a conical bore) expanding slightly at the bottom end to form a bell. The body (called simply *batang*, literally 'long straight object') is made from one piece of hardwood (usually jackfruit wood) and the bell-shaped lower end (called *kecopong* or *pangkal*) is a separate piece attached to the body. The instrument is usually ornamented with carvings at the upper and lower ends of the body and occasionally has raised bands between the six or seven finger holes in front and one at the back.[2]

The reed (*pipit*) is made from four pieces of dried leaf of the palmyra palm (*pokok lontar*) which are cut in the shape of a small fan. The four layers of reed are attached with string to a tubular metal (brass or bronze) reed carrier (*mali*). A small brass disc with a hole in the centre (called *caping*) is mounted on the reed carrier and sits just below the reeds (Plates 25 and 26).

The beating reeds are not controlled by the player's lips, but rather, they are fully inserted into the mouth cavity with the player's lips resting against the small disc (Plate 26).

A melody is produced on the *serunai* by means of a circular (or continuous) breathing technique in which the flow of air through the reeds is rarely stopped. The stream of air from the lungs and mouth flows through the reeds and into the tube of the instrument. Periodically the control of the air stream changes from the diaphragm muscle and the lungs to the facial cheek muscles and the mouth cavity. While the air continues to flow from the mouth cavity, which serves as a kind of bellow (Plate 26), the epiglottis opens the wind passage to the lungs and breath is taken through the nose (to refill the lungs). In this way an unbroken melodic line, once begun, rarely stops until a piece comes to an end.[3]

Double-reed pipes, similar in construction to the *serunai* can be found in the Near East, across northern India, and in Thailand, Indonesia, and other parts of South-East Asia. The oboe of the Near East is known as *surnaya* or *surnay* in Persia, *zurna* or *zorna* in Turkey, and *zukra*, *zamr*, or *gaita* in the Maghrib.[4] In northern India the name *zurna* is applicable to the oboe, preserving to some extent the classical Persian name. In Thailand the *pi phat* ensembles[5] include a quadruple-reed pipe known as *pi nai* whose body shape differs from that of the Malay *serunai*.[6] However, for processions, funeral ceremonies, and matches of Thai boxing and fencing, accompanying small music ensembles include a reed pipe called *pi chawa* whose reed and body construction are very similar to the Malay *serunai*.[7]

Membranophones

The Malay *wayang kulit Siam* ensemble includes three kinds of membranophones called *gedumbak*, *geduk*, and *gendang*. Each drum appears in large and small sizes called *ibu* (mother) and *anak* (child), respectively. Alternately, the two sizes may be referred to as *bapa* (father) and *adik* (younger brother, sister, or friend).

The *gedumbak* has a goblet-shaped body constructed from one piece of jackfruit wood (*kayu nangka*) (Plate 27). A membrane of goat hide is stretched over the opening of the drum head using rattan laces which are attached to the skin with small loops of twisted string sewn into the goat hide. The rattan lacing is, in turn, attached to a metal ring located near the neck of the body. Small wood wedges are inserted between the body and metal ring to tighten the laces and skin. The size of the *gedumbak* is not standard from one set to another. The large *gedumbak* is about 45 centimetres long and 22 centimetres in diameter at the drum head; its goblet-shaped body narrows to a diameter of 12 centimetres at the neck of the drum. The *gedumbak anak* is approximately 2–3 centimetres smaller in all dimensions.

Similarly constructed drums are found elsewhere in mainland South-East Asia and the Near East. For example, a drum nearly identical in construction to the Malay *gedumbak* is known as *thon* in Thailand, and *tombak*, *darbuka*, or *darabukka* in the Near East.[8]

One set of *gedumbak* (*ibu* and *anak*) is played by two musicians as shown in Plate 28. The drum is held in a horizontal position on the player's lap and the single membrane is struck by one hand while the other hand is used to cover the open base end. In this manner various timbres of sound are produced. The sounds are onomatopoeic and are called 'dong', 'duh', 'chap', and 'ting'. These mnemonic sounds are used primarily as memory aids in vocalizing and learning to play specific rhythmic patterns on the drum.

The mnemonic sound 'dong' is produced by leaving open the base end of the drum while hitting the head in the centre with one hand (Plate 29). A similarly produced sound, 'duh', is achieved in an identical manner, but the hand is left on the drum head after impact, creating a muffled or damped sound. The mnemonic 'chap' is produced by completely closing the base end of the drum with one hand and hitting the head in the centre with a quick, snap-like motion of the other hand (Plates 30 and 32). The sound 'ting' is produced by closing the base end of the drum with one hand while hitting the head near its rim with fingers of the other hand (Plate 31). The *gedumbak* provides the standard rhythmic patterns for most pieces and acts as the 'pillar' drum of the ensemble.

The *geduk* is a barrel drum which also appears in two sizes, large and small, called *ibu* and *anak* (Plate 33). The larger drum is approximately 40 centimetres in height with a circumference of 95 centimetres at mid-body. The diameter of the heads is about 30 centimetres. The *geduk anak* is usually about 3 centimetres smaller in all dimensions.

Like the *gedumbak*, the body of the *geduk* is carved from wood of the jackfruit tree. The two heads of cowhide are glued and pegged to the body. In the process of construction, only one head is stretched to extreme tautness before it is permanently attached to the body. The other head is also attached with glue and wood pegs, but since this head is not used, no effort is made to stretch the skin. Two long rattan sticks which are attached to one side of the body and extend beyond it serve as the feet of the drum. These feet allow the drum to be propped upright.

As the drum sits upright, slightly tilted and facing the player, it is hit with a pair of wooden sticks (Plate 34). The drumming technique involves, first, a supple movement in the player's wrists and, secondly, a technique which involves a highly raised movement of the upper arm. No mnemonic system is used for the rhythms played on this drum. The two *geduk* often provide rhythmic patterns which complement the standard patterns of the *gedumbak*, and they always provide specific drumming patterns in the pieces which denote violent or strong action in a story. In addition, the *geduk anak* plays a standard rhythmic cadence to signal the conclusion of musical pieces.

The *gendang* is a double-headed drum with a slightly convex wooden body which is again usually made of jackfruit wood. The wooden body itself is somewhat asymmetrical with a slightly larger bulge at one end in comparison to the opposite end. This drum also appears in two sizes, large and small, called *ibu* and *anak*. The *gendang ibu* is about 55 centimetres in length, 30 centimetres in diameter at the large head, and 26 centimetres in diameter at the small head. In addition, the body, at its central point, is about 80 centimetres in circumference. The *gendang anak* is approximately 2 centimetres smaller in all dimensions (Plate 35).

Each drum, then, has two head sizes, one slightly larger than the other. Both heads of the *gendang anak* are made of goat hide, while the large head of the *gendang ibu* is of cowhide and the smaller, of goat hide. The membranes are braced to the body of the drum by circular pieces of split bamboo on which laces of rattan are looped. The Y-shaped laces can be tightened to raise the pitch and change the timbre. Once the laces have been pulled taut, encircling cowhide loops secure the rattan laces in pairs. The *gendang anak* is tuned so that the large head will produce a pitch to match that of the hanging gong of high pitch (the *tawak anak*). The *gendang ibu* is tuned to produce a low damped timbre on the large head.

Both heads of the *gendang* are struck with the hands as the player sits on the floor holding the drum in a horizontal position on his lap (Plate 35). When struck, the *gendang anak* produces two sounds which are represented by the mnemonic sounds 'chap' (small head) and 'ting' (large head). (It is the pitch of 'ting' which is often tuned compatibly with the high-pitched hanging gong.) The mnemonic 'chap' is produced by damping the large head with one hand, while the small head is hit in the centre with the upper palm and fingers of the other hand (Plates 36 and 37). The sound 'ting' is produced by hitting the large head of the *gendang anak*, near its rim, with the fingers of the hand (Plate 38). The *gendang ibu* produces the sounds 'chap' (also called 'pak') and 'duh' with a playing technique similar to that of the *gendang anak* (Plates 39, 40, and 41). Because of the difference in the size of the two drums, however, the timbres of the mnemonic 'chap' are slightly different.

Various forms of this Malay drum are found throughout South-East Asia. Jaap Kunst, in his work on Javanese musical instruments, describes conical- and barrel-shaped drums with two heads and tuning straps which are known as *kendang* in Java and Bali. Elsewhere in the Malay Archipelago, they are called *gendang, gondrang,* or *ganrang*.[9]

In about one-third of the pieces in the *wayang kulit Siam* repertoire, the *gendang anak* functions as an ornamenting drum, filling in the empty beats (or the beats of rest) in the standard rhythmic patterns played on the *gedumbak*. In a few pieces, however, the two *gendang* are the only drums played. Most of these pieces have been borrowed from the *mak yong* and require singing by the *dalang*.

Idiophones

The idiophones of the *wayang kulit Siam* ensemble function as markers of time within the musical system. The largest is called *tetawak* or *tawak* and consists of two large bossed gongs usually made of bronze (Plate 42).[10] The diameter of the gongs from one ensemble to another can range from 40 to as large as 60 or more centimetres. The gongs are deep-rimmed with thick walls, and with a boss in the centre of the face of the gong. The set of two gongs is usually suspended by rope from the roof beams of the theatre or from a wooden stand. The gongs are held secure by two cross-sticks about 50 centimetres long on which the rope supporting the gongs is wound. Traditionally hung inside each gong are small strips of cloth and raw thread, while a small amount of water is placed at the inside base of each instrument. These items' carry ritual importance according to Kelantanese belief.

When hit on the boss with a padded beater, the gongs produce a high pitch and a low pitch which are referred to as *anak* and *ibu*, respectively. The tuning of the gongs is not standardized from one ensemble to another; however, the important factor is the highness and lowness of pitch in a single pair of gongs. The tonal interval of the two pitches generally ranges from that of a third to a fourth.

The large gongs of good quality are made of bronze and some Malay musicians claim that these most likely came to Malaysia from Java and Sumatra. Neither bronze making nor gong forging is known and practised in Malaysia today. However, gong casting using iron or brass still exists, and it is not uncommon to find gongs of all sizes cast of iron or shaped from large metal barrels.

Another set of idiophones called *canang* consists of two small bossed gongs set on cross-strings on a wooden rack. The diameter of the gongs may range from 15 to 20 centimetres. Very old *canang* (more than 100 years old) are pot-shaped bronze gongs with a boss in the centre of the gong. Newer *canang* made in the twentieth century are fashioned from iron or brass with a very shallow rim and boss. The shallow-rimmed gongs are usually strung on to rattan strips which are attached to a wooden rack (Plate 43). Because of the scarcity of bronze gongs of the proper size and pitch, those of the iron variety are commonly found in ensembles throughout Kelantan since at least the 1970s.

The two *canang* produce a high pitch and a low pitch when hit on the boss with a padded beater, and, like the *tetawak* pitches, the higher *canang* pitch is called *anak* while the lower pitch is referred to as *ibu*. The tuning of the *canang* is again not standardized, and the interval between the high- and low-pitched gongs may range anywhere from a whole step to a sixth. Ideally, an attempt is made to match the pitch of the *canang ibu* with that of the high-pitched *tetawak* (but with one octave displacement).

The final idiophone of the ensemble is known as the *kesi* which usually consists of two pairs of small hand cymbals (Plate 44). The *kesi* are made of bronze or iron and are about 10 centimetres in diameter. They appear in the shape of a small disc with a raised cup-like protrusion in the centre. A small hole in the centre enables a chord to be passed through each piece of metal to connect the pairs together. One (or more than one) pair of *kesi* is attached to a flat piece of wood, and a second pair is held in the player's hands and is struck on to the first pair (or pairs).

It is reported that other types of instruments have been used in place of the small hand cymbals. One of these is called *keline* and it has been described as a slab of iron attached, near the centre of the slab, to a frame or wood. The slab is then hit on each end with a metal beater.[11] A variation of this instrument is a slab of bamboo supported on a wooden frame and hit on either end with a beater.

The playing technique on the cymbals produces two kinds of sounds, damped and undamped. To achieve an undamped sound, the pair of cymbals which is held in the hands is struck on to the second pair and immediately raised after impact (Plate 45). If the pair of *kesi* held in the hands is struck on to the second pair and held in place at the position of impact, a muffled, damped sound is produced (Plate 46). In many pieces of music, these two characteristic sounds of the *kesi* occur simultaneously with the two pitches of the *canang*, the undamped *kesi* with the *canang anak* and the damped *kesi* with the *canang ibu*.

Hand cymbals similar to the Malay *kesi* are found in various sizes throughout mainland Asia, for example, in Buddhist rituals of Tibet and China and in theatrical ensembles. Smaller hand cymbals similar in construction to the *kesi* are used by southern Thai theatrical ensembles and are called *ching*.[12]

The orchestra, then, is composed of ten instruments and normally requires a maximum of ten players. The ensemble can, however, function with fewer players if necessary. During a performance, the players are seated on the floor of the *panggung* behind and in specific relation to the *dalang*'s location. Various seating arrangements are possible and are determined by the *dalang* himself.[13]

The final piece of sound-producing equipment, though not recognized and referred to as a musical instrument, is the *pemetik*, the cueing device. The *pemetik* is a wooden clapper placed during a performance at the *dalang*'s knee (Plate 47). It is constructed of two pieces of narrow board about 50 centimetres long. The two pieces of board are attached at one end and are held slightly apart by a spring device which is secured between the two boards. To cue the orchestra to begin and end a piece, to change tempo, and to create sound effects (especially during battle scenes), the *dalang* produces a loud clap by hitting the *pemetik* with his knee.

The Musicians

The group of musicians who comprise the orchestra is known as the *panjak*. As noted earlier, the maximum number of members, excluding the *dalang*, is ten (one player to an instrument). However, the troupe can and usually does function with fewer members. The players of the *geduk* and *gendang* often double on those instruments with one person each playing one *geduk* and one *gendang*. Occasionally, the *tetawak* player also plays the *kesi*. If doubling of this kind occurs, the total number of members is seven. However, one of the musicians is usually obligated to serve as an aid to the *dalang* during the performance, supplying those puppets stored out of reach of the puppeteer. Thus, it is very difficult to function with only seven members, and the usual number is from eight to ten persons.

The troupe is an exclusively male group. Traditionally, women do not play musical instruments of the *wayang kulit* orchestra nor those of other theatrical orchestras.[14] They tend to take other roles in the performing arts. In the *mak yong*, for example, the primary performers are women who are the principal singers, dancers, and actors on stage. In the *joget gamelan* (court dance) tradition of Terengganu, women are the dancers, while men play the instruments of the gamelan. Women frequently are spirit mediums (*bomoh*), and it has been said that a woman *dalang* was once quite popular in the Tumpat District.

The *wayang* troupe is a mobile group. Most musicians play regularly for a single *dalang*, and are attached to that *dalang* by association with his troupe and his preferred musical style. It is common, however, for a musician to take an occasional job playing for another *dalang* when time permits. If one *dalang* does not have a full complement of musicians, which is often the case, he may borrow a drummer or gong player from the troupe of another *dalang* who is a friend. The 'borrowed' musician has the option to play or not, depending upon whether he has the time, whether he knows the musical style of the other *dalang*, and whether he has the approval of the *dalang* for whom he regularly plays. If two *dalang* are long-standing friends and their style of performance is similar, then frequent borrowing of musicians occurs.[15]

A musician is usually able to play the music for several different musical–theatrical genres of the area, including the *main puteri*, *gendang silat*, *mak yong*, and *manora*.[16] The *wayang* musicians commonly take occasional jobs playing for any other musical–theatrical genre in which they are skilled. For example, both the *serunai* and *gendang* players of Dalang Hamzah's troupe are highly skilled players of the music which accompanies *silat* (the Malay art of self-defence) and both musicians are frequently invited to perform for *silat* competitions in their local villages.

Although *wayang kulit* musicians are paid professional performers, their work as musicians is always a secondary occupation. Most musicians in the Tumpat District sustain themselves by *padi* planting or by fishing and vegetable farming. Their income as musicians is very low and is supplemental to their primary source of income. The amount earned from any one show may be only a few dollars which cannot adequately support a family.[17] In addition, the *wayang kulit* is seasonal and is performed only from March until September or October in a given year. Consequently, a man's supplemental income as a musician is viable only during part of the year.

In the *wayang kulit* troupe of Dalang Hamzah bin Awang Amat, only the *dalang* was, for many years, a full-time performer.[18] The *serunai* player of this troupe has worked as a pedicab (*beca*) driver during the day, while the main *gendang* and *geduk* players are farmers. Another drummer and student *dalang* in the troupe is a *padi* farmer who has to further supplement his income by doing handicraft work. Other musicians work in the batik industry or do jobs in the villages or towns. Economic, social, and other pressures often force many musicians to leave the *wayang kulit*, and this fact is increasingly true through the early 1990s.

Musicians begin to learn their art at a very early age. As young boys, they frequently sit inside the *panggung* to watch a performance. If the interest and inclination are present, they may eventually join a particular troupe, sitting in to imitate and play along with an experienced member of the troupe (Plate 48). Instances arise, too, in which adult men who are recruited by a *dalang* to learn to play the musical instruments later become members of the troupe. The *dalang* and his experienced musicians become the teachers and, in this situation, several newcomers learn in a group.

The first instruments learned are the *canang*, *tetawak*, and *kesi*. The parts played on these instruments are basic and essential to the understanding of the framework of the particular pieces of the *wayang* repertoire. These same parts also teach the student about rudimentary principles of time organization and rhythm which prepare him to progress to the drum parts. The student who always learns in the context of ensemble performance may spend several months to a few years mastering the *canang*, *kesi*, and *tetawak* parts for all pieces of the *wayang* repertoire. When the *dalang* feels the student is competent enough to play all the gong parts, he is allowed to begin learning one of the drum parts which may be either the *gedumbak* or *geduk*. Again, the student is taught by rote, imitating an experienced player. The *geduk* parts in the *wayang kulit Siam* pieces are few in number, and if a student shows a particular flair for the style of drumming on *geduk*, he will be allowed to pursue his study on that drum prior to learning the *gedumbak*. However, learning to play the *gedumbak* is essential, and once a student has learned to play this drum, it is felt that he indeed knows and understands the pieces of the *wayang* repertoire. By the time a musician is considered skilled (*pandai*) in playing the *gedumbak*, one can assume that he knows all the patterns played on the gongs and all the rhythmic patterns played on the drum for the entire *wayang kulit Siam* repertoire.

The final drum a student learns to play is the *gendang* which is played in interlocking style with the *gedumbak* or with another *gendang*. The small-sized *gendang* supplies the patterns of rhythmic complement as well as rhythmic ornament to the central *gedumbak* part. Consequently, it is essential to know not only the basic *gendang* patterns, but also the *gedumbak* rhythmic patterns in order to appropriately execute the various kinds of timbrel embellishments possible on the *gendang* for each piece in the *wayang kulit Siam* repertoire.

The final instrument studied by a student is the *serunai*. It is probably the most technically difficult instrument to play and few musicians and *dalang* have the ability to become good *serunai* players. Although the *serunai* player is able to play most other instruments of the ensemble with some degree of accuracy, not all musicians (nor *dalang*) are able to play the *serunai* with a high degree of competency. Ideally, all trained *wayang* musicians should know how to play all parts for all pieces on all instruments. In practice, however, very few know the *serunai* and there is a tendency to specialize on given instruments such as the *gendang* or *gedumbak*. In Dalang Hamzah's troupe, a once regular *gendang* player was given the *tetawak* part for a short period of time one night during a performance. He soon relinquished the gong beater to the regular gong player because he himself felt he was making too many mistakes. He had not played the *tetawak* for a long time and did not remember the parts any longer. He had become a specialized drummer and was considered an expert *gendang* player by his peers.

All *dalang*, too, should be able to play all instruments of the *wayang* ensemble with some degree of skill, for it is traditionally his responsibility to serve as teacher as well as leader of his troupe. Since the 1970s, however, most *dalang* know how to play only one or two instruments. They cannot dictate specific musical style to their musicians and they cannot teach. Limited musical knowledge on the part of the *dalang* is often the reason why he may not have a constant, full complement of musicians, for he is unable to train new performers to replace those who pass away or leave his troupe.

The *wayang* musicians are able to make and repair their own musical instruments. They are paid for their services and, within their ranks, musicians are recognized as expert players of music (*ahli muzik*) or expert drummers (*ahli gendang*). A particular hierarchy prevails with regard to the status of the musicians within the community of performing *wayang kulit* artists. The *serunai* player, for example, is the closest in rank to the *dalang*, for he has most likely studied for almost as long a period of time as the puppeteer. In many troupes, the *serunai* player is able to perform the prologue to the *wayang kulit*, and he may even have aspirations to become a *dalang* himself.[19] The *gedumbak* and *geduk* players are next in rank with the *gendang* players following behind them. The *tetawak*, *canang*, and *kesi* players are the most poorly paid and carry the lowest status in the *wayang kulit* ensemble.

The ensemble, then, is composed of a group of men who have most likely played musical instruments since childhood. The process of learning the music for *wayang kulit* (or for other musical–theatrical genres) takes place in the traditional rote method and it takes many years before a student becomes highly skilled in his art. Today social or economic conditions often force musicians to abandon their musical activity or to move from one location to another. The lengthy learning process, coupled with the general mobility of musicians, on the one hand, is often cause for concern on the part of the *dalang*, for it is ultimately the responsibility of the *dalang* to keep his troupe together. The mobility and versatility of the musicians, on the other hand, is one factor which ensures an adequate supply of musicians not only for the *wayang kulit* but for other theatrical and musical genres as well.

1. In the state of Kedah, the *wayang kulit* orchestra consists of one *serunai*, one stick-hit *geduk*, two *gedumbak*, one pair of *ching* (finger cymbals), and one pair of small knobbed gongs in a wooden rack. See also Ku Zam Zam Ku Idris, 'Alat-alat Muzik dalam Ensembel Wayang Kulit, Mek Mulung, dan Gendang Keling di Kedah Utara' [Musical Instruments in the Shadow Play, *Mek Mulung*, and *Gendang Keling* Ensembles of North Kedah], in Mohd. Taib Osman and Wan Kadir Yusoff (eds.), *Kajian Budaya dan Masyarakat di Malaysia*, Kuala Lumpur: Dewan Bahasa dan Pustaka, 1983.

2. Jeanne Cuisinier, *Le Théâtre d'ombres à Kelantan*, 3rd edn., Paris: Gallimard, 1957, p. 59, and Henry L. Balfour, 'Report on a Collection of Musical Instruments from the

Siamese Malay States and Perak', in *Fasciculi Malayanses: Anthropological and Zoological Results of an Expedition to Perak and the Siamese Malay State 1901–2 (Anthropology, Part IIa)*, London: Williams & Norgate for the University of Liverpool Press, 1904, pp. 10–11. Cuisinier describes the *serunai* as having seven front stops; Balfour reports on two *serunai* in the collection of musical instruments in the Pitt Rivers Museum at Oxford, England: one with six front stops, and the other with seven. All *serunai* examined by the author in Kelantan during 1976–8 exhibited seven front stops and one at the back.

3. David Morton, *The Traditional Instrumental Music of Thailand*, Berkeley: University of California Press, 1976, p. 151. Morton describes an identical breathing technique in performance on the Thai *pi nai* shawm.

4. Curt Sachs, *The History of Musical Instruments*, New York: W. W. Norton & Co., Inc., 1940, p. 248, and William P. Malm, *Music Cultures of the Pacific, the Near East and Asia*, 2nd edn., Englewood Cliffs, NJ: Prentice-Hall, Inc., 1977, p. 62.

5. Malm, *Music Cultures*, p. 123. The *pi phat* bands of Thailand are percussion-dominated ensembles of gongs, xylophones, and the *pi nai* oboe. The ensembles are heard mainly as accompaniment to official state ceremonies and during dramatic presentations.

6. Dhanit Yupho, *Thai Musical Instruments*, translated from the Thai by David Morton, Bangkok: Department of Fine Arts, 1960, pp. 709–71. The *pi nai* is constructed of a thick, convex teakwood body at its middle section which tapers and then slightly expands at each end.

7. Morton, *Traditional Instrumental Music*, pp. 149–60. 'Chawa' is the Thai word for Java, and from this terminology Morton suggests the Thai probably adopted the instrument from Java, possibly during the Ayutthaya Period (fourteenth to fifteenth centuries), the same time the *klong khaek* (Malay *kendang*) was adopted by the Thais.

8. Dhanit, *Thai Musical Instruments*, pp. 37–42, and Malm, *Music Cultures*, pp. 63–4.

9. Jaap Kunst, *Hindu–Javanese Musical Instruments*, The Hague: Martinus Nijhoff, 1968, p. 40.

10. The term *tawag(k)* refers to the large hanging, bossed gongs used by people in Sabah and Sarawak in the northern part of Borneo. In Lombok and Bali the large bossed gongs are referred to as *tawa'-tawa'*; cf. Tilman Seebas, *An Anthology of South-East Asian Music: Panji in Bali I*, Kassel: Baerenreiter-Musicaphon BM 30 SL 2565, Commentary on the recording.

11. Mohd. Ghouse Nasaruddin, 'Musik Ethnik Malaysia', in *Bahasa, Kesusasteraan Kebudayaan Melayu*, Kuala Lumpur: Kementerian Kebudayaan, Belia dan Sukan Malaysia, 1976, pp. 167–207. Neither this instrument nor its bamboo variant was seen by the author during her field research in Kelantan.

12. Morton, *Traditional Instrumental Music*, p. 123.

13. Shahrum bin Yub, 'The Technical Aspects of the Kelantan Malay Shadow Play Theatre', *Federation Museums Journal*, New Series, XV (1970): 43–75. Shahrum's article deals with the construction of the *panggung* and the seating arrangements for both the *wayang Siam* (*wayang Kelantan*) and *wayang Jawa* (*wayang kulit Melayu*) types of shadow play as performed in Kelantan.

14. The author's teachers and informants often commented that women certainly had the ability to learn to play musical instruments, but they usually had little time or no inclination to do so.

15. This was also the case in the 1970s with Dalang Hamzah bin Awang Amat and Dalang Yusuf Hassan of Kampung Mesira.

16. *Main puteri* is an exorcism ritual performed by a *bomoh* (shaman) to the accompaniment of music. *Gendang silat* is music performed to accompany the Malay art of self-defence (*bersilat*). *Mak yong* is the Malay dance-drama, and *manora* is the Thai dance-drama.

17. Shahrum bin Yub, 'The Kelantan Malay Shadow Play Theatre', p. 65. Shahrum reports that in 1927 a typical payment to a *dalang* for one complete performance would be RM3.50. The *serunai*, *geduk*, and *gedumbak* players would receive RM2.50 and all others RM1.50. In 1972 Sweeney reports somewhat higher figures, and by the late 1970s musicians and *dalang* were still earning approximately what they earned in 1972.

18. Dalang Hamzah's situation as a full-time performer of *wayang kulit* through the 1970s was rare among *dalang*, for most puppeteers supported themselves (and still do in the 1990s) by working at other occupations. For Dalang Hamzah, however, the performance of *wayang kulit* was his only source of income, supplemented by making leather puppets and musical instruments which were sold to other less skilled *dalang* in the area and also to town shops selling handicraft objects to tourists. During the past several years, Dalang Hamzah has also supplemented his income by teaching his theatrical art in the Performing Arts Programme of the Universiti Sains Malaysia in Penang, and today he survives economically by practising traditional medicine and the *main puteri* healing ritual.

19. In Dalang Hamzah's troupe, the main *serunai* player is the highest paid musician who occasionally performs the prologue to the shadow play. He is probably the most generally skilled musician in the group and is highly competent on most other instruments of the ensemble.

4
The Musical Style

Musical Form

The Gongan *and Principles of Musical Form*

TEMPORAL cycles, which are marked internally at specific points by specific gongs and at the end by the lowest-pitched gong of an ensemble, are referred to as gong units or *gongan*.[1]

The phenomenon of musical systems based on temporal cyclicality is found in many parts of South-East Asia, notably in the gamelan music of Indonesia where gong ensembles find a high degree of sophistication. In Peninsular Malaysia, with its close affinity to the island areas of South-East Asia, it is not surprising to find a similar orientation to the organization of musical time and to the structuring of musical pieces, particularly in an ancient theatrical–musical genre such as the *wayang kulit*.

In the music of the Malay *wayang kulit Siam*, the *gongan* is predicated on a 2-level stress unit which is realized by the two pitches of the *canang* (gong chime): the first level is weak and is represented by the high-pitched gong tone (called the *anak* or child), while the second level is strong and is represented by the low-pitched gong (called the *ibu* or mother). The 2-level stress unit is manifested by two beats or pulses in the music (that is, a single stroke of a high pitch and a low pitch) and is repeated, always in multiples of two, throughout a given *gongan*. This 2-level stress unit is sometimes vocalized by the Malay musicians as 'ding-dong' in which 'ding' is the weak pulse and 'dong' is the strong pulse. The main pulse or beat in the music is always 'dong'. In effect, a gong unit is composed of a given number of repeated 2-level stress units (the total number of beats in the unit always being a multiple of two) and it is marked at the end by the lowest-pitched gong, the *tawak ibu*.

Each *gongan* has a specific musical form which is generated by the process of subdivision of the temporal cycle in a binary way, that is, first into halves, then quarters, eighths, sixteenths, and so on. Each subdivision of the gong unit is usually marked by the sound of a specific gong in the orchestra. The first division of the *gongan* (into halves) is always marked by the *tawak anak* (the high-pitched hanging gong), while the end of the temporal unit is marked by the *tawak ibu* (the low-pitched hanging gong). The successively smaller levels of subdivision are marked by the pitches and timbres of the *canang* and the *kesi* (cymbals). Specific gongs marking specific points (or beats) in the temporal unit give a definite structure to the unit. A *gongan*, once established, is unchanging and is infinitely repeatable in any given piece of music. These are the primary structures which determine the shape or form of a piece of music and serve as the framework in which melody, rhythmic patterns, and puppet movement take place.

To illustrate the *gongan* and its divisive and binary characteristics, the simplest and smallest gong unit in the *wayang kulit* repertoire is shown in Example 1 (in both a cyclical and a linear representation). The 8-beat cycle is first marked at its end by the *tawak ibu* gong tone (symbolized as **G** in the example). It is then divided in half by the *tawak anak* gong tone (symbolized as **g**) at beat 4. The low pitch of the *canang ibu* (shown as D) and the damped timbre of the *kesi* further subdivide the cycle into fourths by sounding on beats 2, 4, 6, and 8. Finally, the high-pitched *canang anak* (d) and undamped *kesi* subdivide the cycle into the smallest segments, into eighths, by sounding on beats 1, 3, 5, and 7.

The same 8-beat *gongan* can also be illustrated by writing out the beats in a linear fashion, showing each successive level of subdivision on a higher plane as in Example 2. The linear representation shows that the subdivision is manifested by the sounding of specific gongs in specific registers, each successively smaller division marked by a higher-pitched gong tone than the preceding one.[2] This phenomenon has been termed 'polyphonic stratification' and is found in many other kinds of music played by gong ensembles in South-East Asia. In Example 2 the lowest-pitched gong (the *tawak ibu*, symbolized as **G**) marks the end of the cycle on beat 8. The next higher gong (the *tawak anak*, **g**) marks the mid-point of the cycle, dividing it in half. The small gong in high register (the *canang ibu*, D) and the damped *kesi* (x) subdivide the

EXAMPLE 1

The Structure of the 8-beat *Gongan*

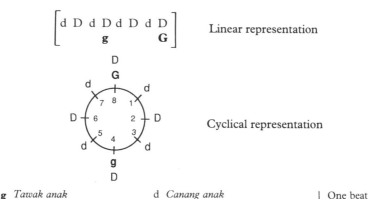

g *Tawak anak*	d *Canang anak*
G *Tawak ibu*	D *Canang ibu*

| One beat

EXAMPLE 2

The Subdivision of the 8-beat *Gongan*, Illustrated on Linear Planes
and Showing the 2-level Stress Unit

Levels of subdivision:

(3) *Canang anak* (weak	c		c		c		c			High pitch in	
stress, d) and	d		d		d		d			high register	
undamped *kesi* (c)	.	.	.	.	.	.	.	.			
	1	2	3	4	5	6	7	8			

(2) *Canang ibu* (strong		x		x		x		x		Low pitch in	
stress, D) and		D		D		D		D		high register	
damped *kesi* (x)	.	.	.	.	.	.	.	.			

(1) *Tawak anak*				**g**					High pitch in	
									low register	
	.	.	.	.	.	.	.	.			

Tawak ibu (**G**),								**G**	Low pitch in	
signifying the	.	.	.	.	.	.	.	.	low register	
complete *gongan*										

Beats: 1   2   3   4   5   6   7   8

gongan into quarters by marking the end of each quarter unit. Finally, the highest-pitched gong (the *canang anak*, d) and the sharp, ringing timbre of the *kesi* (c) mark the subdivision of the cycle into eighths.

Another important feature of the *gongan* is that in all pieces of music, the gong units are concatenated, and the point of connection is always at the gong tone of the *tawak ibu*. The stroke on this gong, marking the end of one cycle, is also the beginning point, marking the start of another cycle. In the Malay shadow play music, the process of concatenation usually involves gong units of the same structure in any single piece of music. However, *gongan* of different structures, chained together in specific ways, are also found in a small part of the repertoire. Once a given gong unit or a number of different gong units are structurally established in a given piece of music, neither the *gongan* nor the succession in which they are played deviates from the established order. The repetition of a specific gong unit is unchanging in a given piece of music.

Expansion and Contraction of the Gongan

In Javanese gamelan and other music using the gong unit as the basis of musical form, the expansion and contraction of the gong unit occurs in a given piece as part of the developmental process in the actual performance of the music.[3] In any given gong unit, the ratio of main beats to one stroke on the low gong can double, thereby expanding the *gongan* or, conversely, the ratio can decrease by half, thus contracting the gong unit.

In the musical pieces of the Malay shadow play, the processes of expansion and contraction of the gong unit do not take place during the performance of a piece; rather the ratio of main beats per low-pitched gong tone always remains constant. However, these processes of expansion and contraction of the gong unit can be seen as developmental (or compositional) processes which have occurred at some past time, and it is through these processes that the specific fixed musical structures have been derived.

In the composition of the pieces for the *wayang kulit*, the expansion of a gong unit occurs when each beat of the 2-level stress unit becomes two beats, yet maintaining the sequential weak–strong stress. In this expansion process, the time interval between each beat in a gong unit is made greater, allowing for the insertion of more 2-beat units between each of the main downbeats. The greater time interval between each beat allows for the insertion of more downbeats and, thus, the ratio of main beats to one stroke on the low-pitched gong doubles in the new 'expanded' gong unit.[4]

In contrast, the contraction of a gong unit occurs when the 2-beat stress unit (vocalized as 'ding-dong' and representing weak–strong stress) contracts and becomes one unit or beat, either a weak or a strong beat in the gong cycle. This process is illustrated in Example 3 using a 16-beat musical form which is characterized by a high-pitched gong tone at beats 8, 12, and 14, and a low-pitched gong tone on the final beat of the unit. The weak and strong beats in the unit are marked by the high- and low-pitched *canang* gong tones, respectively (noted as d and D in Example 3). Through the process of contraction, each of the successive 2-level stress units of the 16-beat cycle contract into a single unit, alternating weak (noted as d) and strong (noted as D), and the result is an 8-beat gong unit. This smaller gong unit maintains the 2-level stress unit as well as the same internal structure as the larger unit with specific gong tones marking the same relative position in both the 16- and the 8-beat *gongan*. This 8-beat gong unit shown in Example 3 occurs in many pieces of the *wayang kulit* repertoire as a cadential gong unit or as part of a larger repeated gong cycle.

EXAMPLE 3
Derivation of an 8-beat *Gongan* through the Process of Contraction

Tawak:							g			g		(g)		G
Beats: 1	2	3	4	5	6	7	8	9	10	11	12	13	14	15 16

16-beat
gongan: d D d D d D d D d D d D d D d D

8-beat
gongan: d D d D d D d D

Beats: 1 2 3 4 5 6 7 8

Tawak: g g (g) G

g *Tawak anak*	**d** *Canang anak*	↓ Contracts to
G *Tawak ibu*	**D** *Canang ibu*	**(g)** Gong optional

The Basic Musical Forms

The musical pieces of the Malay shadow play are based on eight basic gong units, each of a specific structure. An additional five gong units are derived from the basic units (all the musical forms are summarized in Appendix 3). The additional five structures are made up of two or more basic gong units which are played in a specific order and, thus, they may be referred to as compound musical forms.

The shortest of the basic musical forms is a *gongan* of 8 beats in which the high and low tones of the *canang* alternately mark every pulse as the weak and strong running beats in the gong unit. As shown in Example 1, the high-pitched *tawak anak* subdivides the cycle in half by sounding on beat 4 while the low-pitched *tawak ibu* marks beat 8 of the unit. This short 8-beat *gongan* serves as the musical form for a great number of pieces which accompany two different kinds of puppet movement, that is, the movement of battle and other strong action, and the movement of walking by specific characters. For example, the action of fighting, descent from and ascent to the heavens, and other strong action is accompanied by the pieces entitled 'Perang' [Battle], 'Dewa Panah Turun' [Descent of the Demigods with Bows and Arrows], and 'Dewa Panah Perang' [Battle of the Demigods with Bows and Arrows]. In contrast, the action of walking by specific characters or character-types takes place with the pieces 'Berjalan' [Walking] for refined characters, 'Pak Dogol' (for the character so named), 'Dewa Keluar' [Demigods Appear], and 'Seri Rama Masuk Istana' [Seri Rama Enters the Palace]. In addition, this 8-beat *gongan* is the musical form for the signalling piece called 'Bertabuh' [Beating the Drums].

Two other larger musical forms are essentially expansions of the 8-beat gong unit, each larger form retaining the same structural configuration of gong tones as the 8-beat *gongan*. The first of these larger forms is 16 beats in length. As in the 8-beat *gongan*, the *canang* high and low pitches mark all weak and strong stresses, respectively, while the *tawak anak* subdivides the gong cycle in half with a single stroke of the gong on beat 8. The *tawak ibu* marks the end of the unit by sounding on beat 16 (Example 4). This musical form is found in the *lagu* 'Maharisi' (used for walking by the old sage), as well as the pieces entitled 'Bertukar Dalang' (for changing the *dalang*), 'Dewa Berjalan' (for walking by the demigods), 'Binatang Berjalan' (for the appearance and walking by animals), 'Orang Darat' (for the appearance of country bumpkins), 'Main Alun' or 'Menggali' (for the echoing of sound or the action of digging), 'Pari' (for fairies walking), 'Menghendap', 'Menghindar' or 'Memburu' (for the actions of crouching in ambush, averting danger, or hunting), 'Peran Hutan' (for the appearance of the Jungle Clown), and 'Sang Kaki' (for the appearance of the character by that name).

The second of the larger musical forms generated by the expansion of the basic 8-beat *gongan* is 32 beats in length (Example 4). Just as in the 8- and 16-beat gong units, the *tawak anak* marks the subdivision of this large cyclical unit into halves (at beat 16) while the *tawak ibu* sounds only on the final beat. Each of the 32 beats is further marked as weak and

EXAMPLE 4

Gongan of 16 and 32 Beats Generated by the Expansion
of the Basic 8-beat Gong Unit

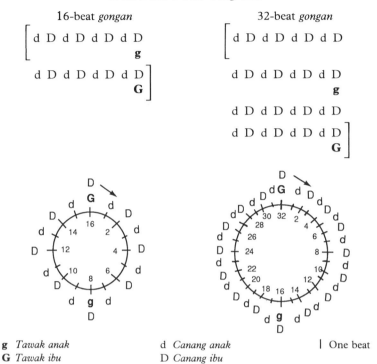

16-beat *gongan*

$$\begin{bmatrix} d\ D\ d\ D\ d\ D\ d\ D \\ \qquad\qquad\qquad \mathbf{g} \\ d\ D\ d\ D\ d\ D\ d\ D \\ \qquad\qquad\qquad \mathbf{G} \end{bmatrix}$$

32-beat *gongan*

$$\begin{bmatrix} d\ D\ d\ D\ d\ D\ d\ D \\ d\ D\ d\ D\ d\ D\ d\ D \\ \qquad\qquad\qquad \mathbf{g} \\ d\ D\ d\ D\ d\ D\ d\ D \\ d\ D\ d\ D\ d\ D\ d\ D \\ \qquad\qquad\qquad \mathbf{G} \end{bmatrix}$$

g *Tawak anak*	d *Canang anak*	∣ One beat
G *Tawak ibu*	D *Canang ibu*	

strong stress by the high and low pitches, respectively, of the *canang*. This 32-beat musical form is the basis of only one piece in the repertoire, the piece entitled 'Seri Rama Keluar' [Seri Rama Appears] from the prologue to the shadow play.

In each of these three formal structures, the *kesi* serve to support and reinforce the weak–strong stress pattern in the gong unit by sounding in unison with the *canang*. A ringing or undamped timbre played on the *kesi* sounds in unison with the *canang* high pitch (weak stress or all odd-numbered beats in the *gongan*) and a damped timbre on the *kesi* is heard simultaneously with the *canang* low pitch (strong stress or all even-numbered beats in the gong unit).

The fourth of the basic forms in the music system is a *gongan* consisting of 16 beats, with the two *canang* gong tones marking the 2-beat weak–strong stress pattern in the gong unit (Example 5). In this 16-beat unit, however, the *tawak anak* subdivides the gong cycle into half and then into quarters by sounding at beats 8 and 12. A unique characteristic of this *gongan* is that the gong tone marker one would expect at beat 4 is deleted. The high-pitched *tawak anak* also sounds at beat 14 which serves as a signal for the approaching end of the cycle at beat 16. As in all musical forms of the Malay shadow play repertoire, the low-pitched *tawak ibu* is played on the final beat of the gong unit. This musical form appears in the piece 'Maharisi' as the cadential gong unit in the piece.

EXAMPLE 5
The 8-beat and 16-beat Cadential *Gongan*

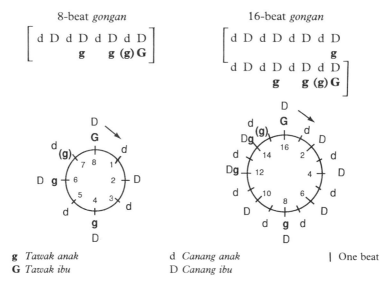

g *Tawak anak*   d *Canang anak* | One beat
G *Tawak ibu*   D *Canang ibu*

Note: Parentheses indicate the gong tone may or may not occur.

Its function as a cadence unit also applies to its contracted version, that is, an 8-beat gong unit. The 8-beat unit is also shown in Example 5 where the identical configuration of gong tones is evident between the large and the small gong unit. The 8-beat cadential unit serves as an ending *gongan* for nearly all pieces in the repertoire based on an 8- or 16-beat *gongan*. Therefore, the 8-beat cadential *gongan* is not repeated, but occurs only one time in any given piece of music.

Identical in structure to the 16-beat cadential *gongan* (and probably derived through the process of expansion of this 16-beat unit) is a musical form of 32 beats. As in most pieces of the Malay shadow play repertoire, the *canang* and the *kesi* are struck on each of the running beats of the gong unit marking the weak–strong stress pattern. The high-pitched *tawak anak* once again serves as the principal form-generating instrument, and in this 32-beat *gongan* it is played on beats 16, 24, 28, and 30, subdividing the gong unit into halves, quarters, eighths, and sixteenths, respectively. The low-pitched *tawak ibu* maintains its usual function of sounding on the final beat of the gong unit (Example 6). This particular 32-beat structure is the musical form for the piece 'Dewa Panah Berjalan' [Demigods with Bows and Arrows Walk] from the prologue, as well as the frequently heard piece 'Hulubalang' [Warriors]. This piece for the warriors appearing and parading has a variant (in dramatic function and drum rhythmic pattern) which is entitled 'Hulubalang Menyembah' [Warriors Pay Homage].

A 16-beat *gongan* borrowed from the Malay *mak yong* dance-drama is the basis of a piece entitled 'Sedayung' which, in fact, is the piece 'Sedayung Pak Yong' from the dance-drama repertoire. In this musical

EXAMPLE 6
The 32-beat *Gongan* Derived from the 16-beat Cadential Gong Unit

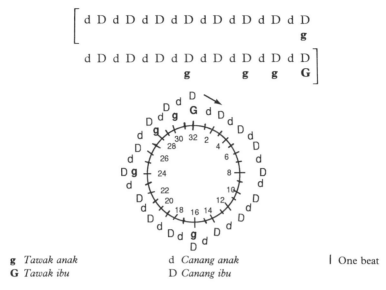

| **g** *Tawak anak* | **d** *Canang anak* | **|** One beat |
| **G** *Tawak ibu* | **D** *Canang ibu* | |

form, the *tawak anak* subdivides the 16-beat gong unit into halves, fourths, and eighths by sounding on beats 4, 8, 12, and 14, while the *tawak ibu* is played only on beat 16, marking the end of the cycle. Unlike the *mak yong* version, however, in the shadow play rendition of this *gongan*, the *canang* and *kesi* mark the running beats as in all other shadow play pieces.[5]

An expanded version of the 'Sedayung' musical form is used for a number of sung pieces in the shadow play. The expanded form is 32 beats in length with the same arrangement of gong tones as the 16-beat form (Example 7). In this larger form, the *tawak anak* sounds on beats 8, 16, 24, 28, and 30, thereby subdividing the *gongan* into halves, quarters, eighths, and sixteenths, while the *tawak ibu* marks only beat 32. The *canang* fulfils its usual function, marking every weak and strong beat in the gong unit. The *kesi*, however, serve to reinforce the strong beats by producing a ringing, undamped timbre on the upbeat just preceding each strong beat. The ringing timbre is immediately followed by a damped timbre on the downbeat of the strong stress simultaneously with the low-pitched *canang ibu*. During the final quarter of the gong unit (beats 24–32), the *kesi* part often increases in density by sounding on the upbeat and downbeat of every main pulse in the music. This 32-beat form (based on the 'Sedayung' form) is the basis for the sung tunes called 'Saudara' [Friend, Companion] and 'Kijang Mas' [Golden Deer] borrowed from the *mak yong* dance-drama, as well as the piece 'Menyembah' [Paying Homage], an excerpt of which is transcribed in Appendix 4. These sung pieces are collectively referred to as the *lagu menyanyi* in which the melody is alternately carried by the *dalang* (who sings the appropriate text for the given dramatic situation in the story) and the *serunai* player.

EXAMPLE 7

The 16-beat *Gongan* of the *Lagu* 'Sedayung' and Its Expanded Form, the
32-beat *Gongan* of the *Lagu* 'Menyanyi' in Slow Tempo

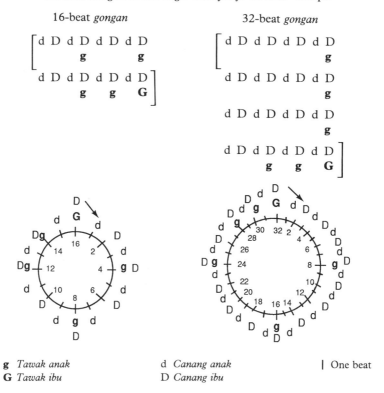

| **g** | *Tawak anak* | d | *Canang anak* | | One beat |
| **G** | *Tawak ibu* | D | *Canang ibu* | | |

The Compound Musical Forms

All of the compound musical forms, summarized in Appendix 3, are
constructed from the basic single *gongan* forms. The first of these is based
on the 8-beat gong unit (Example 1). The basic 8-beat gong unit occurs
consecutively three times followed by the 8-beat cadential gong unit
(Example 5). This arrangement of 8-beat gong units makes up a cyclical
chain of four *gongan* (or a total of 32 beats) which is repeated in the
same sequence throughout a piece of music. The pieces using this
musical form are entitled 'Tidur' [To Sleep], 'Mengulit' [To Lull], 'Mandi'
[To Bathe], 'Minum' [To Drink], 'Baca Surat' [To Read a Letter], and
'Memetik Bunga' [To Pick Flowers]. Melodically, rhythmically, and
formally, these are all the same piece, but the text changes according to
the requirements of the dramatic situation at any given time in the story.

Another 32-beat compound musical form is based on the joining of
two *gongan*. The first is the 16-beat basic gong unit (shown in Example 4)
which is joined to the 16-beat cadential *gongan* (shown in Example 5).
The resulting cyclical, repeated unit of 32 beats is the structural
foundation for two pieces heard only occasionally in the shadow
puppet play. Both pieces are referred to as 'Barat' which literally means

'West'. However, in this case, the term refers to a piece to accompany the action of travelling, or moving from one location to another by both male and female characters. The two 'Barat' pieces are distinguished as 'Barat Anjur' or 'Barat Lambat' [Slow Barat], featuring a very slow tempo, and 'Barat Patah' [Broken or Disconnected Barat] (*patah* being a modifier applied to the style of the drum rhythmic patterns) in a faster tempo. It is possible that the inspiration for these two forms of 'Barat' finds its origins in the *mak yong* musical repertoire.

A compound musical form of 48 beats is found in the pieces entitled 'Berkhabar' [To Give News or Information], 'Khabar Wayang' [News of the Shadow Play], or 'Tanya Khabar' [To Ask for News]. These pieces retain the same formal structure, rhythmic patterns, and melody; only the text changes to reflect the given dramatic situation during which the piece is sung. They are frequently heard in the performance of a shadow play and feature the singing of lyrics by the *dalang* alternating with highly embellished melodies played on the *serunai anak*. The repeated, cyclical musical form for these pieces consists of the 16-beat basic *gongan* (shown in Example 4) played twice and followed by the 16-beat cadential gong unit (shown in Example 5). These three gong units are played consecutively to form a single repeated structure of 48 beats in length which is the musical form for the vocal pieces asking for (or giving) news.

A second 48-beat musical form consists of, first, the 32-beat *gongan* for the piece 'Hulubalang' (shown in Example 6) linked to the 16-beat cadential gong unit (shown in Example 5). This repeated musical form of 48 beats serves as the basis for two pieces of contrasting dramatic function, that is, conveying an emotion and the parading movement of a special character. The piece which evokes an emotion is called 'Menangis' (or 'Teriak', in the Kelantan dialect) and is used to express extreme sadness and even weeping. In fact, the signal to begin the piece is an exaggerated sob given by the *dalang* which prompts the orchestra to begin an ad lib beating on the instruments (referred to as *gertak perkakas*, literally 'rattling of the instruments'). Immediately following the *gertak perkakas*, the piece is rendered in a considerably fast tempo. The unique feature of 'Menangis' is that its musical form is played only one time as a fixed, and not a repeated, unit. In contrast, the same 48-beat musical form, repeated as a cyclical event in time, serves as the basis for the piece entitled 'Maharaja Rawana'. This piece accompanies the parading by King Rawana, who is the major adversary of the hero-prince Seri Rama in the *Ramayana* story. This story, however, is rarely performed and, consequently, the musical piece is heard infrequently.

A final compound musical form consists of four gong units linked together to comprise a 56-beat repeated cycle. The 16-beat basic *gongan* (Example 4) is played two times, followed by the 16-beat cadential *gongan* (Example 5), which is then followed by the 8-beat cadential gong unit (Example 5). This formal structure of 56 beats serves as the basis for a piece called 'Khabar dan Dayang', the piece for giving news to or by a maiden. Closely related to the piece 'Berkhabar' in dramatic function, drum rhythmic patterns, melody, and musical form, information is conveyed in 'Khabar dan Dayang', with lyrics sung by the *dalang* and a highly ornamented melody carried by the small-sized *serunai*.

Rhythm

The emphasis on the divisive nature of the musical forms in Malay *wayang kulit* music, seen in the organization of musical beats, is no less important in the element of rhythm, particularly as manifested in the drum rhythmic patterns of the musical pieces. Although some triplet figures are to be found in some pieces of the repertoire, the rhythm is overwhelmingly duple in nature. The four square orientation of musical time and rhythm in Malay shadow play music, organized in meters of 2, 4, or 8 beats, is commonly found in many other genres of traditional Malay music of the Peninsula and, indeed, in much of the music throughout both island and mainland South-East Asia.[6] The use of triple meter is not found in Malay *wayang kulit* music, but the use of hemiola, or the juxtaposition of 2 beats in one part played simultaneously with 3 beats in another part, occurs to some extent.

Another important feature of rhythm in traditional Malay music, including that of the *wayang kulit*, is the use of accent of some kind at the end of rhythmic patterns. Again, this end-accented feature of the music is also found in many other South-East Asian genres.[7] The use of agogic accent, volume, timbre, or additional percussive elements on the second beat of a 2-beat unit, and the increase in intensity of accent at the end of each successive 2-beat unit in a rhythmic figure, ultimately finds the greatest accent, and hence the greatest importance, on the final beat of a complete rhythmic pattern. This hierarchical-like occurrence of accent, then, provides the 'end accent' feature which is the norm in the composition of rhythmic patterns in a piece of music.

A final important feature, related to rhythm and to the way in which it is produced on drums, is the use of an 'interlocking' style in the performance of the rhythmic patterns. In many pieces of the Malay shadow play, no single drummer produces a rhythmic pattern which is complete in itself. Instead, each drummer of the orchestra plays specific timbres at specific times to generate one complete rhythmic pattern. This phenomenon, the use of 'interlocking' or 'shared' parts among two or more performers, can be likened to hocket technique in which each performer produces a specific pitch at a specific time to produce one complete, composite melody. This technique, by which melodies and drum rhythmic patterns result, is found throughout South-East Asia in the *angklung* and other ensembles of Indonesia, and in the gong and bamboo tube ensembles of northern Borneo and the southern Philippine islands. It finds a high degree of development in the music of the *gender wayang* of the Balinese shadow play and also in the drumming of the Malay *wayang kulit*.

1 *Wayang kulit Melayu* flat leather puppets.

2 *Canang* and players in the *wayang kulit Melayu*.

3 *Gendang* and player in the *wayang kulit Melayu*.

4 *Rebab* and player in the *wayang kulit Melayu*.

5 *Rebab* detail (body, neck, and bow).

6 A typical village *panggung* for the *wayang kulit*, temporarily erected for a performance. (The screen has not been put in place.)

7　A permanent village *panggung* for the *wayang kulit*, showing the slanted screen.

8　Interior of the *panggung* prepared for the start of a performance.

9   Puppets with two movable arms: Pak Dogol and Wak Long.

10   Pak Dogol with a movable lower jaw, and Wak Long with both upper and lower jaws articulated.

11 Puppets with two movable
arms: *orang darat.*

12 Seri Rama, hero-prince of
the *Ramayana.*

13 Laksamana, prince and
brother of Seri Rama.

14 Maharisi Kala Api and the
balai.

15 King Rawana, the major
   adversary of Seri Rama.

16 Siti Dewi, wife of Seri
   Rama.

17 *Dayang* in traditional and
contemporary dress.

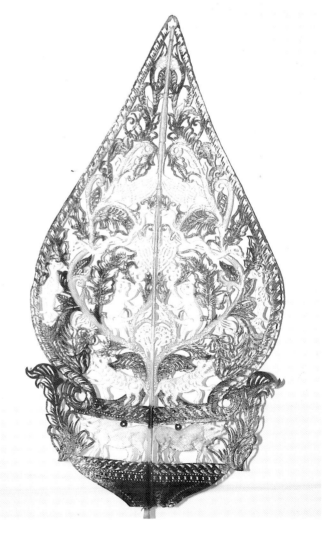

18 *Pokok beringin.*

19 Opening scene of the
'Dalang Muda' prologue:
pokok beringin with
Maharisi Kala Api (*centre*)
and the two *dewa panah*
(*left and right*).

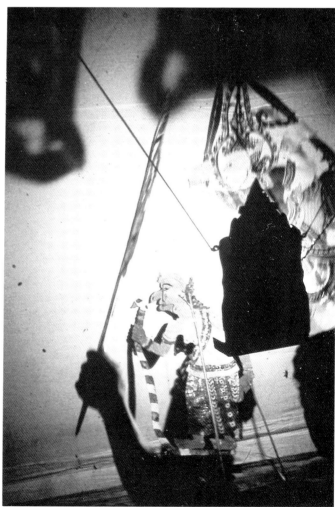

20 The two *dewa panah*
descend from the heavens.

21 The two *dewa panah* in battle at the screen.

22 Hanuman Kera Putih.

23 Seri Rama gesticulating before his Chief Minister and warriors.

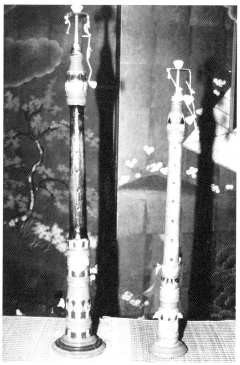

24 *Serunai ibu* and *anak*.

25 Reed (in two double layers of dried palm leaf) and lip disc for the *serunai*.

26 *Serunai*, position of mouthpiece and fingers; note the puffed cheeks typical of the circular breathing technique.

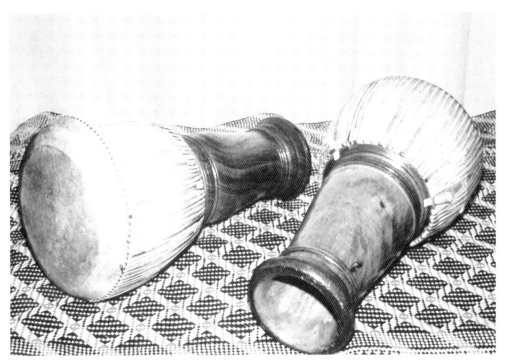

27   *Gedumbak ibu* and *anak*.

28   *Gedumbak*, playing position.

29 *Gedumbak*, hand positions for production of mnemonic 'dong'

30 *Gedumbak*, hand positions for production of mnemonic 'chap'.

31 *Gedumbak*, hand positions for production of mnemonic 'ting'

32 *Gedumbak*, hand position closing base end in production of mnemonics 'chap' and 'ting'.

33 *Geduk ibu* and *anak*.

34 *Geduk ibu*, playing position.

35 *Gendang anak* and *ibu* with players.

36 *Gendang anak*, large head damped in production of mnemonic 'chap'.

37 *Gendang anak*, hand position for production of mnemonic 'chap'.

38 *Gendang anak*, hand position for production of mnemonic 'ting'.

39 *Gendang ibu*, hand position on impact in production of mnemonic 'duh'.

40 *Gendang ibu*, large head damped in production of mnemonic 'chap'.

41 *Gendang ibu*, hand position on impact in production of mnemonic 'chap'.

42 *Tetawak* with player.

43   *Canang* with player.

44   *Kesi.*

45 *Kesi*, impact of cymbals in production of undamped sound.

46 *Kesi*, impact of cymbals in production of damped sound.

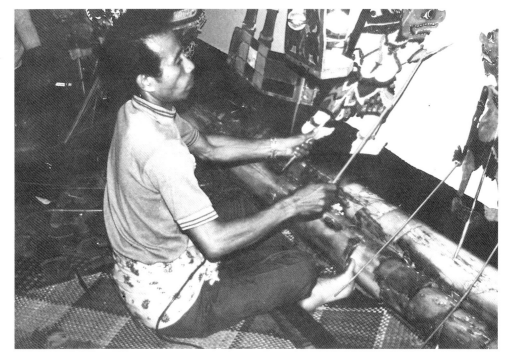

47　*Pemetik* at the *dalang*'s right knee.

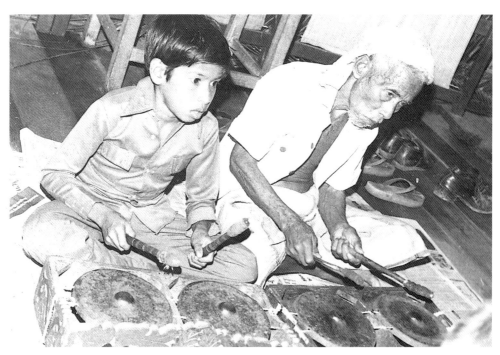

48　The old teaching the young in traditional rote practice.

The Gedumbak *Rhythmic Patterns*

The *gedumbak* has been referred to as the 'pillar' drum in the orchestra, for it provides the basic rhythmic patterns for over half the pieces of the repertoire. It is found most commonly with the *gendang anak* (small-size *gendang*) which provides the patterns of rhythmic complement interlocking with the basic *gedumbak* patterns. However, to depict strong or violent action in the drama, the *gedumbak* appears with the stick-hit *geduk*, as in the pieces 'Perang', 'Bertabuh', and in the descent and battle of the *dewa panah* in the prologue.

The *gedumbak* is always played as a set of two drums (large and small sizes) by two players, and the rhythmic patterns are played either in unison or with the smaller *gedumbak* anticipating the beats of the larger drum by one-half or one-quarter of a beat. The musicians on this drum utilize three different timbres of sound which are vocalized (as a memory aid in the learning process) as 'chap' (a high, sharp clap-like timbre), 'dong' (low, loud), and 'ting' (high, soft). These mnemonic sounds are played on specific beats to create specific rhythmic patterns or parts of patterns.

In the *wayang kulit* repertoire, the *gedumbak* patterns are 8, 16, 32, or 48 beats in length. However, the building blocks of the longer patterns are various short 4-beat rhythmic figures. In effect, a number of identical or contrasting 4-beat figures are repeated to make up the longer patterns.

The 8-beat *gedumbak* patterns are built using 4-beat rhythmic figures, each 4-beat figure ending simultaneously with a gong tone at the half or full *gongan* in a given piece of music (if it is based on the musical form of an 8-beat gong unit). Some frequently heard pieces of this type are 'Perang', 'Berjalan', 'Bertabuh', 'Pak Dogol', and 'Dewa Keluar'. The most common type of 8-beat pattern is iterative (outlined as *a, a*) in which the first 4-beat rhythmic figure is repeated to make up the 8-beat pattern as shown in the piece 'Pak Dogol' in Example 8. Other 8-beat *gedumbak* patterns are characterized by a contrasting pair of 4-beat figures (outlined as *a, b*) such as that which occurs in the opening of the piece 'Perang' and as shown in the standard cadence pattern which concludes most pieces.

The *gedumbak* rhythmic patterns of 16 beats occur in the framework of a 16-beat gong unit or in two 8-beat gong units. The structure of the *gongan* does not dictate the internal composition of the rhythmic pattern itself, but it sometimes influences the placement of specific rhythmic figures within the total 16-beat pattern. The 16-beat patterns, for the most part, accompany the walking movement of various character-types as well as the actions of digging, hunting, and crouching in ambush. These types of puppet movement are represented in pieces such as 'Maharisi', 'Binatang Berjalan', 'Orang Darat', 'Dewa Berjalan', 'Menggali', and 'Memburu'.

Similar to the 8-beat *gedumbak* patterns, all 16-beat patterns may be segmented into four 4-beat figures. The most common type of pattern

EXAMPLE 8
The Main Types of 8-beat *Gedumbak* Patterns

(i)   *a, a* form in the piece 'Pak Dogol'

(ii) *a, b* form in the standard cadence pattern

is one in which two contrasting 4-beat figures alternate positions in the total 16-beat pattern (outlined as *a, b, a, b*), shown in the excerpt from the piece 'Binatang Berjalan' in Example 9(i). The first 4-beat figure *a* is characterized by rests on the weak stresses (the first and third beats), while the 4-beat figure *b* emphasizes the low, loud 'dong' timbre. In this *a, b* pattern where the 4-beat figure *b* ends simultaneously with a gong tone, the order of the two 4-beat rhythmic figures reinforces the subdivision of the 16-beat gong unit at the half *gongan*.

In contrast, another type of 16-beat pattern is made up of three different 4-beat figures in which the internal identical figures are bounded by two different contrasting figures (outlined as *a, b, b, c*), shown in the excerpt from the piece 'Maharisi' in Example 9(ii). In some instances the repetition of figure *b* occurs over the gong tone (at the half *gongan*) and, thus, provides rhythmic continuity rather than delineation in relation to the structure of the 16-beat gong unit. Another main type of the 16-beat *gedumbak* pattern is essentially through composed, whereby four different 4-beat rhythmic figures make up the total pattern (outlined as *a, b, c, d*), shown in the excerpt from the piece 'Dewa Berjalan' in Example 9(iii).[8] It is interesting to note that in both the 'Maharisi' and 'Dewa Berjalan' examples, and in many other pieces as well, the 4-beat rhythmic figures follow the weak–strong stress pattern of the gong unit in which rests occur on the first and sometimes the third beats, while specific timbres are always played on the second and fourth beats.

The longer *gedumbak* rhythmic patterns of 32 and 48 beats in length occur in only three pieces, and although the number of tunes using these rather long patterns is small, the importance of at least one of the pieces

EXAMPLE 9
The Main Types of 16-beat *Gedumbak* Patterns

(i) *a, b, a, b* form in the piece 'Binatang Berjalan'

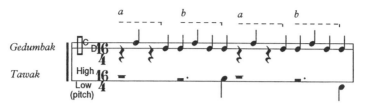

(ii) *a, b, b, c* form in the piece 'Maharisi'

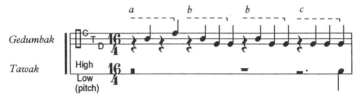

(iii) *a, b, c, d* form in the piece 'Dewa Berjalan'

in the repertoire is considerable. One of those musical numbers heard frequently in performance today is the tune for the parading movement of the warriors, entitled 'Hulubalang'. It is based on the 32-beat *gongan* shown in Example 6. The piece is composed of a 32-beat *gedumbak* pattern which, like all other drum patterns, may be segmented into short 4-beat rhythmic figures. As shown in Example 10, the complete rhythmic pattern, in its basic form, takes shape in two large formal parts (beats 1–16 and 17–32) which contrast in the use of timbres, but still maintain some degree of motivic relationship from one 4-beat rhythmic figure to another. Most of the 4-beat figures are characterized by weak stress on the first and third beats (usually by a musical rest) and strong stress on the second and fourth beats (notated in Example 10, and vocalized as 'rest-ting-rest-chap'—beats 1–4, or 'rest-dong-rest-dong'—beats 13–16). While the first part of the overall pattern (beats 1–16) uses extensive repetition of material (outlined in the form *a, a, a, b*), the second part of the pattern (beats 17–32, outlined as *c, d, b, b*) uses some contrasting rhythmic motifs along with the repetition of the *b* material from the first part of the overall pattern. Here, as in many other rhythmic and melodic patterns of the *wayang kulit* repertoire, the basic principles of contrast

EXAMPLE 10

The 32-beat *Gedumbak* Rhythmic Pattern for 'Hulubalang'

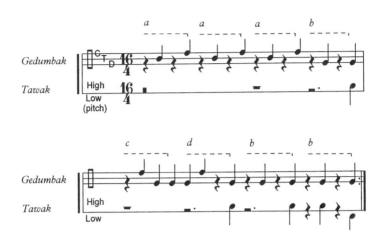

and repetition give diversity and interest, as well as cohesiveness, to the musical fabric.

Another piece using a lengthy *gedumbak* rhythmic pattern is known by the title 'Maharaja Rawana'. This piece is important in the repertoire from a historical perspective, for it is used only for the appearance of the character King Rawana, the major adversary of Seri Rama, in the *Ramayana* story. The piece itself is identical to 'Hulubalang' noted above, but with an appended 16-beat cadential pattern. The thematic relationship in the 4-beat rhythmic figures of this piece is maintained within the cadential pattern itself, and between it and the 32-beat pattern shown in Example 10.[9]

The final piece using a 32-beat *gedumbak* pattern is also important historically in the repertoire, for it is the piece to accompany the appearance of the hero-prince Seri Rama. The piece, known as 'Seri Rama Keluar', is still heard occasionally because it is used in the opening 'Dalang Muda' prologue. In the *gedumbak* rhythmic pattern for this piece, four contrasting 4-beat figures make up the first half of the total pattern (in the formal scheme outlined as *a, b, c, d*) which is repeated to comprise the full 32-beat pattern.[10]

As the preceding examples have shown, the rhythmic patterns of the *gedumbak* drum are built within the parameters of the gong unit in a given musical piece, and are typically 4, 8, or 16 beats in length. The 2-level stress pattern of the gong unit (the weak–strong stress) governs the occurrence of a similar pattern found in the drumming. The musical rests in a given rhythmic pattern usually occur on the weak beats of a gong unit, while the specific timbres of sound produced on the drum occur on the strong beats; and when no rests occur in a given rhythmic pattern, the lower or louder timbres (called 'dong' and 'chap') are predominant on the strong beats of the *gongan*.

While the *gedumbak* rhythmic patterns are essential to many of the pieces in the *wayang kulit*, the *gedumbak* drumming provides only part of the total picture for the distinctive rhythmic patterns. In several pieces of the repertoire, including the frequently heard tunes 'Pak Dogol', 'Binatang Berjalan', 'Menggali', 'Bertukar Dalang', and 'Hulubalang', the small-sized *gendang* provides the interlocking rhythmic patterns with the two *gedumbak*.[11] The interlocking style of performance on these different drums results in the complete, distinctive rhythmic patterns for each of the respective pieces in the repertoire.

The *gendang anak* is a double-headed, tuned drum on which the player produces two basic timbres vocalized as 'chap' (a loud, sharp sound produced on the large drum head) and 'ting' (a somewhat resonant, low timbre produced on the small drum head). Like the rhythmic patterns of the *gedumbak*, the patterns played on the small *gendang* may also be broken down into 4-beat rhythmic figures. When the *gendang anak* provides the interlocking patterns with the *gedumbak*, the timbres played on the *gendang* always occur on the weak beats of the pattern (and hence on the weak beats of the gong unit of the piece). As shown in Example 11 in the piece entitled 'Pak Dogol', the *gendang anak* provides specific timbres on beats 1, 3, 5, and 7 (the weak beats of the *gongan*), while other specific timbres on the *gedumbak* occur on beats 2, 4, 6, and 8 (the strong beats of the gong unit). This patterning is typical of ensemble drumming on the *gedumbak* and *gendang* and clearly indicates the orientation of the *gendang anak* interlocking drum patterns to the weak beats of the gong unit (see also the pieces 'Hulubalang' and 'Binatang Berjalan' in Appendix 4).

EXAMPLE 11

The *Gedumbak* and *Gendang* Interlocking Rhythmic Pattern for 'Pak Dogol'

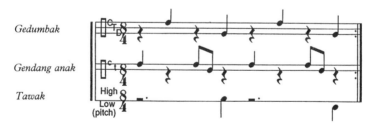

The Gendang *Rhythmic Patterns*

In a number of pieces of the *wayang kulit* repertoire, only the two double-headed *gendang* of the ensemble are used to provide the percussive rhythmic patterns in the music. These pieces include the tune 'Berjalan', all types of 'Barat', 'Sang Kaki', and the vocal pieces 'Tidur', 'Mengulit', 'Mandi', 'Minum', 'Baca Surat', 'Memetik Bunga', 'Menangis', 'Sedayung', 'Menyembah', 'Berkhabar', 'Tanya Khabar', 'Khabar Wayang', and 'Khabar dan Dayang'. In all of these pieces, only the two *gendang* (large and small sizes) are used to play the percussive rhythmic patterns in the style of 'interlocking' or 'shared' parts. It is in these pieces which feature *gendang* drumming that the technique of 'shared' part-playing reaches a very high degree of sophistication in Malay shadow play music. In these pieces, each *gendang* is played by a single drummer who produces specific timbres by hitting the tuned drum heads in specific ways and in selective locations on the surface of the tightened skin. It has already been noted that the *gendang anak* produces two timbres vocalized as 'chap' and 'ting', but the larger drum also produces two different timbres referred to as 'chap' or 'pak' (a high, sharp sound) and 'duh' (a low, loud timbre). Although the same mnemonic, 'chap', is used to denote the specific timbre produced on both drums, the timbre itself is slightly different between the large and the small drum because of the difference in the size of the drums and the thickness of the drum heads. Using these four basic timbres, then, the two drummers spin out interlocking rhythmic patterns in basic as well as highly ornamented versions. As a given piece begins, the drum patterns are likely to be played in a basic, unornamented way, rather similar to the version which would be taught to a beginning drummer. As the given piece progresses, however, the improvisatory interplay between the two drummers becomes evident and, using an increasingly greater number of timbrel ornaments (in Malay, *bunga*), the interlocking drum patterns may deviate far from the established basic pattern, but they always return to it in the end.

Similar to the *gedumbak* patterns, the *gendang* patterns may be 8, 16, 32, 48, or 56 beats in length, and all occur in the context of specific musical forms (or gong units). All of the basic patterns, however, are based on various 4- or 8-beat rhythmic figures. The patterns tend to be end-weighted so that a given rhythmic figure or pattern ends simultaneously with a stroke on the *tawak*.

Each of the pieces known as 'Berjalan' and 'Barat Cepat', for example, are built using 4-beat rhythmic figures. These are repeated (in the formal scheme *a, a*) to form a complete 8-beat pattern which occurs within the framework of an 8-beat gong unit. Thus, each of the 4-beat figures ends with a gong tone at the half and full *gongan* as shown in Example 12. As can also be seen in the excerpt from the piece 'Berjalan', the mnemonic sounds 'chap' and 'ting', played by two different drummers on the *gendang anak* and *gendang ibu*, generate one complete (or resultant) 8-beat rhythmic pattern which is distinctive to this piece.

Other *gendang* patterns are 16 or 32 beats in length and may be segmented into 4-beat figures or, more typically, 8-beat figures. In the pieces entitled 'Tidur', 'Mengulit', 'Baca Surat', 'Mandi', 'Minum', and 'Memetik Bunga', two contrasting 4-beat figures are used to build a complete 32-beat rhythmic pattern. The complete rhythmic pattern for these pieces is played in the time framework of the compound musical form consisting of three 8-beat basic *gongan*, concluding with one 8-beat cadential *gongan* (as described in Examples 1 and 5) so that the 4-bar figures making up the pattern always end with a gong tone (at the point of the half or full *gongan*). The two different 4-beat figures, shown in the basic rendition in Example 13, are played in a specific order which

EXAMPLE 12

The Basic Rhythmic Pattern for 'Berjalan'

(i) 'Interlocking' parts in the basic rhythmic pattern

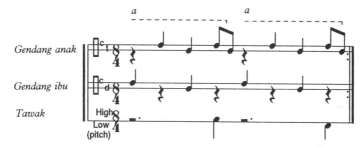

(ii) 'Resultant' rhythmic pattern

can be outlined in a 4-part form as *aa, aa, aa, a^{1}b* (or in the larger overall 4-part patterning as *A, A, A, B*).

One of the most important pieces in the *wayang kulit* repertoire using *gendang* rhythmic patterns built on 8-beat figures is the piece entitled 'Menyembah' (alternately, 'Kijang Mas' or 'Saudara', as borrowed from the *mak yong* dance-drama). It is a sung piece in a very slow tempo with

EXAMPLE 13

The Basic 4-beat *Gendang* Resultant Rhythmic Figures for 'Tidur'

(i) 4-beat figure *a*

(ii) 4-beat figure *b*

the two *gendang* drummers playing an interlocking rhythmic pattern within the time framework of a 32-beat gong unit (the expanded form of the 'Sedayung' *gongan*) as shown in Example 7 and in Appendix 3. The 32-beat rhythmic pattern for the piece is generated, first, by a repetition of a given 8-beat figure and, secondly, by a single statement of a cadential 8-beat figure (shown as figures *a* and *b*, respectively, in Example 14). The order of occurrence of the two 8-beat figures, *a* and *b*, may be represented in the large 4-part formal scheme of *a, a, a, b*,

EXAMPLE 14

The 8-beat *Gendang* Rhythmic Figures for 'Menyembah'
(Also Known as 'Kijang Mas' and 'Saudara')

Pattern I: The basic, unornamented rhythmic figures.
(i) Figure *a*

(ii) Figure *b*

Pattern II: The ornamented 8-beat rhythmic figures (a frequently heard version). The individual interlocking *gendang* parts are shown in the transcription of the piece in Appendix 4.

(i) Figure *a*

(ii) Figure *b*

identical to the large overall patterning in the piece 'Tidur'. This antecedent–consequent patterning (*a, a, a, b*) is also found in some *kendang* patterns in a specific drumming repertoire of Javanese gamelan music.[12]

Each of the 8-beat rhythmic figures for this vocal tune in slow tempo occurs in the time frame of a quarter-*gongan* (or 8 beats) and, consequently, the last beat of each 8-beat figure occurs simultaneously with a gong tone. This end-weighted nature of each 8-beat pattern is increasingly emphasized as the gong tones become more frequent (occurring on beats 24, 28, and 32) in the cadential 8-beat figure *b*. The basic, unornamented version of the 8-beat figure *a* is always characterized by a musical rest (no drum timbres) on the first and third beats of the figure and, in order to allow adequate time for the *dalang* to complete his text and melody, the rest on beat 1 is often sustained for several seconds as the drummers wait for the completion of the first several words of the textual phrase sung by the puppeteer. As the piece progresses, however, the tempo increases and a highly ornamented drumming style ensues with many timbrel ornaments filling in the rests and, hence, providing greater rhythmic density as shown in Pattern II of Example 14.

The remaining examples of 32-beat *gendang* rhythmic patterns built on 8-beat figures are simpler, iterative structures. For example, the *gendang* patterns for the two pieces 'Barat Patah' and 'Barat Anjur' consist of an 8-beat rhythmic figure played a total of four times to fill in the time of the 32-beat compound musical form (the *gongan*) in which they occur.[13] The 'Barat Patah' presents an example of a rhythmic pattern described as 'broken' or 'disconnected' (*patah*) in which the flow of rhythmic activity is interrupted (or broken) by a musical rest on every fourth downbeat in the 8-beat figure (Example 15, beats 4 and 8). In addition, this 8-beat figure is characterized by the steady alternation of the timbres occurring on each downbeat and upbeat played on the large and small *gendang*. As seen in Example 15, the *gendang ibu* provides drum timbres on each main beat of the pattern, while the *gendang anak* alternates the 'chap' and 'ting' timbres only on the upbeat of each main pulse. The 'disconnectedness' of the 8-beat figure, then, is also evident in the alternation of timbres from one drummer to the other.

EXAMPLE 15

The Repeated 8-beat *Gendang* Rhythmic Figure for 'Barat Patah',
Shown in Interlocking Parts

Finally, the additional interlocking patterns of great length (32 beats or more) in the *gendang* repertoire are found in the pieces called 'Berkhabar' (alternately, 'Tanya Khabar' or 'Khabar Wayang'), 'Khabar dan Dayang', and 'Menangis'. The two former musical pieces are used to relate news of some kind while the latter is heard only occasionally for the purpose of conveying extreme sadness. Although the complete patterns are 48 or 56 beats in length, they invariably are based on 8-beat rhythmic figures. In the pieces for relating news, for example, three different 8-beat figures are linked together in specific order to comprise the complete 48- or 56-beat patterns. The distinctive patterning of the three contrasting figures results in a rounded, 3-part design in which a specific 8-beat figure appearing early in the total pattern appears again near the end. In the case of the piece 'Khabar dan Dayang', the repeated 8-beat figure is reiterated a second time at the end of the pattern to generate a considerably long 56-beat *gendang* pattern.[14]

In general, the interlocking rhythmic patterns played on the two *gendang* are spun out using 4- or 8-beat figures which, theoretically, can be broken down further into 2-beat units. The 2-beat rhythmic units find correspondence in the 2-level stress pattern of the gong cycle (the *gongan*). As the 2-beat rhythmic units combine to form the 4- and 8-beat figures, the complete rhythmic patterns in specific formal schemata emerge to form the drum rhythmic material of the musical pieces. As the preceding examples of rhythmic patterns have shown, the main types of formal structures of the patterns are iterative (*a, a*), antecedent–consequent (*a, a, a, b*), and rounded (*a, b, a*). At the beginning of a piece, the tempo typically is slow but gradually increases with each successive *gongan* to a moderate or fast speed. The specific rhythmic patterns are always played in the time framework of specific musical forms (*gongan*), and greater rhythmic density is usually found as the approach is made to the final gong tone of a given gong unit. As the two *gendang* drummers begin to improvise on the basic rhythmic patterns in a given piece of music, the ornamentation becomes increasingly thick and the drummers venture far from the original, basic pattern, but then make a cycle-like return to the basic rendition near the end of the piece. The notion of cyclicality governs the very fabric of the musical texture.

The Geduk *Rhythmic Patterns*

Both the large- and small-sized *geduk* provide patterns of rhythmic complement to the 4- and 8-beat basic rhythmic figures played on the *gedumbak* in the shadow play music. In addition, the *geduk* is heard in ensemble with the small *gendang* only in the standard final cadence pattern used in several pieces of the repertoire. In general, the loud, stick-hit *geduk* rhythmic patterns are used to depict strong or violent action in the drama, or they signal the cadence pattern at the end of a piece.

The rhythmic patterns in *geduk* drumming are based on 2-beat figures

EXAMPLE 16
The Rhythmic Figures in the *Geduk* Pattern (Reverting Type)
from 'Perang'

(i) Figure *a*

(ii) Figure *b*

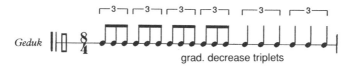

(iii) Figure *c*

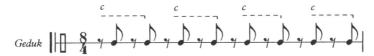

which may be repeated in various ways and combinations to generate short or long patterns, but always keeping within the time framework of the *gongan* in which they occur. The most common type of *geduk* pattern is a reverting form using three different rhythmic figures. The pattern is characterized by the statement of two different rhythmic figures, followed by a third contrasting figure, and a repetition of the two initial figures but in reverse order. The overall formal scheme is *a, b, c, b, a*. Within this reverting formal pattern, each of the figures *a, b,* and *c,* shown in Example 16, may be repeated a number of times to extend the length of the pattern (but always within the context of a half or full *gongan*), and the change from one figure to another is made at the discretion of the drummer who follows the action of the puppets on the screen. In addition to its use in the opening (or signalling) piece called 'Bertabuh', this reverting type of *geduk* pattern is used in all music to accompany battle or other violent action as, for example, in the pieces 'Perang', 'Dewa Panah Turun', and 'Dewa Panah Perang'.

Another type of pattern found in *geduk* drumming is iterative in structure, using a single, repeated rhythmic figure (*a, a, a, a,* and so on) throughout a piece or a section of a piece. The repeated figure may be played on a single *geduk* or it may consist of an interlocking figure played on the *geduk ibu* and *anak* as illustrated in Example 17. Along with the specific *gedumbak* rhythmic patterns, this interlocking *geduk* pattern typically accompanies the actions of descent from or ascent to the heavens, walking by the *dewa panah*, hunting (*memburu*), avoiding danger (*menghindar*), or stalking (*menghendap*).

EXAMPLE 17

The Iterative, Interlocking *Geduk* Pattern from 'Menghendap'

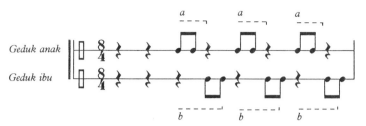

The final type of *geduk* pattern consists of a given rhythmic figure stated three times and concluded by a contrasting figure. Described earlier as an 'antecedent–consequent' form (*a, a, a, b*) commonly heard in *gendang* drumming, this type of pattern is found in *geduk* drumming in only one piece of the repertoire, the tune for the appearance of the country bumpkins ('Orang Darat', notated in Appendix 4). Unlike other *geduk* patterns in which the length is somewhat flexible and extendable by the repetition of the specific rhythmic figures comprising the pattern, the length of the antecedent–consequent pattern and the repetition of the specific rhythmic figures are fixed to make up a full 8-beat pattern. The basic pattern for the piece 'Orang Darat' and one of its variants, shown in Example 18, both maintain the antecedent–consequent structure, although each of the patterns is distinctive in rhythmic composition.

In its function to signal the cadence at the end of a piece, the *geduk* provides cadential patterns in both the iterative and antecedent–consequent types of formal schemes. The iterative type is found in only four pieces of *wayang kulit* music, while all other pieces concluding with a *geduk* rhythmic pattern use the antecedent–consequent type. Used

EXAMPLE 18

The Antecedent–Consequent *Geduk* Patterns from 'Orang Darat'

(i) 'Orang Darat' basic pattern

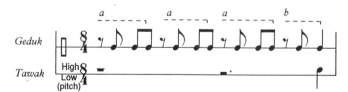

(ii) 'Orang Darat' variant pattern

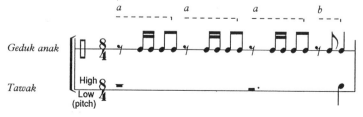

EXAMPLE 19
The Standard *Geduk* Cadential Pattern

extensively as the ending pattern for many pieces of the repertoire, this type is a standard *geduk* cadence pattern. Shown in Example 19, it is always played in the framework of the 8-beat cadential *gongan* and exhibits two important characteristics of *geduk* drumming, that is, drum strokes on the weak beat or upbeat of a main pulse in the music, and conclusion on the penultimate beat of the *gongan*.

Melody

The *serunai* is the only melodic instrument in the ensemble and appears in large and small sizes (called *serunai ibu* and *anak*, respectively) allowing for melodies in both high and low registers. Because of the quadruple reed and other aspects of the physical construction of the instrument, the *serunai* provides a strident, loud, and sometimes raucous sound quality which pierces through and soars above the beating of the drums and gongs. The *serunai* player provides the melody in most pieces of the *wayang kulit Siam* repertoire, and in the sung pieces (*lagu menyanyi*), the *dalang* and the *serunai* player alternate in producing the melodic line of a given piece. The melodies of the various pieces in the repertoire are improvisatory in nature and tend to be highly embellished using many melodic ornaments. Because the *serunai* player uses a continuous (or circular) breathing technique (see Chapter 3), once a melody begins there is rarely a break in the flow of sound until the piece comes to an end. Thus, the unbroken melodic line is a continuous chain of predominantly stepwise melodic contours, long-sustained and vibrato-less single tones (dead tones), and fast moving eighth, sixteenth, and triplet note passages in which melodic ornaments of several types are embedded.

In the purely instrumental pieces, the *serunai* part is intended to beautify a piece rather than provide a unique melody to identify it (the drum rhythmic patterns serve the function of specifically identifying the individual pieces of music in the repertoire). Existing in an oral tradition in which fixed or set versions of pieces are not written down, it is common to find similar melodic contours, figures, and phrases and, in fact, identical melodic phrases used and repeated in several different pieces (*lagu*) in the shadow play repertoire. Some instances of shared melodies may be seen, for example, in the pieces entitled 'Bertabuh', 'Perang', and 'Menghendap' and also in the group of tunes entitled 'Dewa Berjalan', 'Bertukar Dalang', 'Sang Kaki', and 'Menggali'.[15] In both the former and latter groups of pieces, the opening melodic passages are nearly identical and the same melodic figures and phrases are strung together to generate the melody common to the pieces in each group. Another group of pieces sharing identical melodies are 'Hulubalang' (including 'Hulubalang Menyembah') and 'Maharaja Rawana'. Similar, but not identical, melodic phrases and contours appear in the two pieces known as 'Binatang Berjalan' and 'Pari', while another set of similar melodies is used in all the 'Barat' and related pieces.[16]

To exist solely in an oral tradition implies that the musical pieces are not written down in any way. But oral tradition also entails many more factors intrinsically bound up with the experience of the performer and his culture. In the Malay *wayang kulit Siam*, for example, the young musician acquires his musical skills by listening and imitating the older, experienced players of a troupe. The *serunai* player, learning to play the *wayang kulit* melodies, has not only learned by rote without the aid of notation of fixed pieces, he has also absorbed the centuries of musical and melodic traditions of his culture and of the given art form. His experience of learning in an oral tradition is not unlike that of the singers of epics and other oral literature.[17] The melodic formulae of *wayang kulit Siam* music are heard from the time of childhood and are memorized by listening and later by playing the *serunai*. Eventually, the student learns how to put the melodic figures together to form a complete melodic line. The short melodic figures, the longer melodic phrases, the scales, the melodic contours, and the various melodic ornaments become the *serunai* player's musical vocabulary to use in an appropriate order and to manipulate according to the musical grammar dictated by his tradition.

Tonal Vocabulary and Scales

Based on the sung and instrumental melodic parts of the pieces in the *wayang kulit Siam* repertoire, specific scales emerge as important structures in the building of the melodies. Because the *serunai* is still made by hand by local artisans, the length and diameter of the tube varies slightly from one set to another and, consequently, the range of the pitches varies to some degree from set to set. Nevertheless, analysing the melodies played on one specific set of instruments (a *serunai ibu* and *serunai anak*, made as a given pair), it is possible to specify a tonal vocabulary and range considered to be typical for the instrument and for *wayang kulit Siam* musical pieces. As shown in Example 20, the tonal vocabulary for the *serunai ibu* generally encompasses the range of a ninth (*B* to *c*), while that of the small *serunai* is an octave (*F* to *f*). Most tones (or pitches) produced on the instrument approximate the tones of the Western-tempered chromatic scale. However, some *serunai* tones are occasionally slightly sharper or flatter than those of the Western tuning system, and these pitches in the various *wayang kulit Siam* musical pieces are so marked in the following discussion when they occur consistently in the repertoire.

The scalar structures used in the various musical pieces for the *wayang kulit Siam* are 5-, 6-, or 7-tone scales, and most encompass the range

EXAMPLE 20
Tonal Vocabulary of the *Serunai Ibu* and *Serunai Anak*

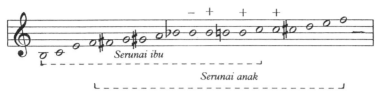

of an octave or less. The majority of scales are gapped and thus include the interval of a minor or major third (approximately), which may be found in first or final (or in some cases, both) positions in the scale. As summarized in Example 21, several of the gapped 6- and 7-tone scales are particularly distinguished by the use of the major third interval (or gap) at the beginning of the scale, while other scales also feature a minor third interval in the final position in the scale. In these scales a core group of five tones is usually predominant in any given melody, and these various pentatonic structures, used frequently in the various pieces, are shown by the use of whole notes (the white notes) in the summary of scales in Example 21.

EXAMPLE 21
Summary of Scales

I. Gapped Scales

Heptatonic

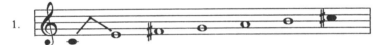

Hexatonic

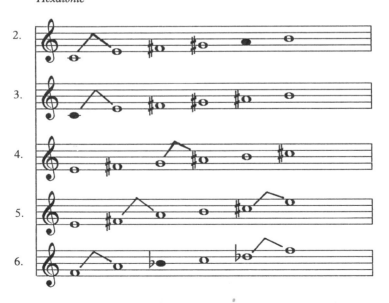

Pentatonic

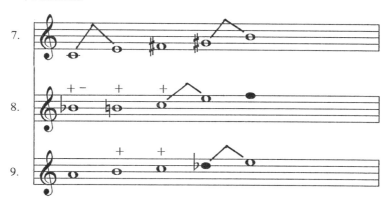

II. Non-gapped Scales

Pentatonic

The majority of the scales are constructed of various series of whole and half tones along with a gap. As shown in Example 21, the gapped 6- and 7-tone scales are notable for the occurrence of a major third interval (approximate) at the beginning of the scale, while some of these scalar patterns also feature two gaps. In the octave scale beginning on the pitch *e* (Example 21, scale no. 5) the two gaps of a minor third (or three semitones) occur at the opposite ends of the scale, and the octave scale on *f* (Example 21, scale no. 6) features two gaps of a major third (four semitones) also found at the opposite ends of the scale. In many pieces built on the scales beginning with the gap of a major third (pitches *c* to *e* in Example 21, scale nos. 1, 2, 3, and 7) the pitch centre is consistently the second scale degree, as is evident in the pieces 'Perang', 'Binatang Berjalan', and 'Pak Dogol', notated in the transcriptions in Appendix 4. In pieces using the octave, gapped scales (Example 21, scale nos. 5 and 6), the pitch centre occurs on the third or fourth scale degree, as in the piece 'Orang Darat' (notated in Appendix 4), based on scale no. 6 with the pitch centre on scale degree 4.

A gapped scale encompassing the range of a sixth and featuring an augmented second (three semitones) found in the middle position in the scale is shown in Example 21, scale no. 4. This hexatonic scale is found in three pieces of the repertoire, including 'Menyembah' (see

Appendix 4) and 'Seri Rama Keluar' (Example 22). Although all the basic pitches of this scale are used in these pieces, certain altered tones are also frequently heard. In the piece 'Seri Rama Keluar', for example, both of the pitches *c#* and *a#* may appear in certain melodic phrases in their natural form. The alternation of the natural and sharped form of these pitches is found throughout the sung passage of the *bilangan* for Seri Rama in the piece 'Seri Rama Keluar'. (The text of the *bilangan* sung by Dalang Hamzah is given in Chapter 2, and the notation of select melodic passages is found in Example 22.)

Of the gapped pentatonic scales in Example 21 (scale nos. 7–9), the scale no. 7 (*c* to *b*, with two gaps in the first and final positions in the scale) is closely linked to the hexatonic scale no. 2 and, indeed, is the pentatonic core most commonly used from the larger scale. Like its parent scale, the pentatonic version retains the range of a seventh as well as a gap of a major third at the beginning of the scale. The remaining gapped, pentatonic scales (scale nos. 8 and 9) show some marked similarities to each other while they contrast greatly with all other scale structures in the repertoire. Both scales, nos. 8 and 9, encompass the narrow range of a fifth (*B*-flat to *f* and *a* to *e¹*), and both include slightly altered pitches and a gap of an approximate minor third (or augmented second) interval at the upper end of the pentachord. Of these two scales, scale no. 8, found in the pieces 'Berkhabar' and 'Khabar dan Dayang', consists of three semitone intervals and a gap of a major third in the middle of the scale. The melodic figures and phrases built on this pentatonic scale focus primarily on the lower tetrachord made up of two semitones and the interval of a third (the relevant pitches are shown in white notes in Example 21). In addition, the first scale degree tends to be unstable, played with many nuances of pitch sometimes slightly flat and at other times slightly sharp. In the 'Berkhabar' melody, this unstable pitch usually occurs as a grace note or as the beginning tone of a slide (or glissando). The slightly sharp feature of the second and third scale degrees is peculiar to this scale and also to the scale for the piece 'Sedayung' (Example 21, scale no. 9) which has been borrowed from the *mak yong* repertoire. The pitch centre of the melodies built on these two narrow-ranged scales is found on scale degree 3.

The two non-gapped scales are narrow in range and are of the pentatonic variety. Of these scales, the pentachord built on the pitch *e* (Example 21, scale no. 10) is derived from the hexatonic scale on *c* (scale no. 2), again indicating the importance of a pentatonic core of pitches found in the 6- and 7-tone scales of the repertoire.

Melodic Phrases and Ornaments

Within the context of a given vocabulary of tones and scales, the *serunai* player and the *dalang* (as vocalist) spin out long lines of melody, using sustained, vibrato-less tones which are performed in sharp contrast to long passages of fast-moving notes with many melodic ornaments. Using excerpts from the *dalang*'s vocal part in the *bilangan* for Seri Rama (performed during the piece 'Seri Rama Keluar' in the 'Dalang Muda' prologue) shown in Example 22, as well as examples from the vocal piece 'Menyembah' in Appendix 4, several basic characteristics of a typical *wayang kulit Siam* melody become evident.

In Example 22, three phrases of text and melody from the piece 'Seri Rama Keluar' have been selected to illustrate the use of specific scale tones and melodic ornaments. The first and second phrases notated in Example 22 (bars 1–3 and 4–7) occur consecutively in the piece, while the third phrase (bars 7 [beats 3–4] to 11) follows somewhat later (compare with the text of the *bilangan* given in Chapter 2). One of the most characteristic melodic ornaments used in the *wayang kulit Siam*

EXAMPLE 22

Excerpts from 'Seri Rama Keluar': The *Dalang*'s Sung Text

music (in both vocal and instrumental forms) is the slide or glissando from one pitch to another. The slide may encompass only a whole tone as in bar 1 of Example 22, or it may span the interval of a third or fourth as in bars 4 and 10 (see also the *serunai* part in the piece 'Berjalan' in Appendix 4). This melodic ornament may be found as a short upward slide to the beginning note of a melodic phrase or it may last through one or more beats in either an upward or downward motion (see Example 22, bars 1, 4, 7, and 10, and the pieces 'Berjalan' and 'Menyembah' in Appendix 4).

In nearly all sung pieces in the *wayang kulit Siam* repertoire, the melodic phrases are generally characterized by passages of repeated tones with no vibrato or tremolo followed by rather long highly ornamented melismata. The melodic contours are generally found in falling or undulating patterns. The melodic phrases constructed in this way essentially follow the textual material. The basic words of a given line from a verse are sung or intoned on only one or two pitches, while an extension of the final sung syllable or a meaningless 'filler' syllable is sung on a long melismatic passage.[18] In Example 22, for instance, the first melodic phrase includes the first complete line of text in the *bilangan* ('hilang royat cerita nak timbul') sung using only two tones, while the meaningless syllable ('ah') is used to sing a lengthy melisma which features the use of sixteenth note motion, altered pitches, tremolos (or wobbles to the pitch below), slides, and the glottal stop. At this point it is interesting to note that the first melodic phrase in Example 22 (bar 1 to bar 3 [beat 1]) is sung in the time of one quarter of a gong unit (the piece 'Seri Rama Keluar' is played using a 32-beat *gongan*), while the following melisma fills the time of 16 beats or the next two quarter units of the *gongan*. One more melodic/textual phrase of 8 beats completes the duration of the 32-beat gong unit used for this piece.[19] The final melodic/textual phrase notated in Example 22 (bars 7–10) illustrates, again, the use of a single tone to sing the main text ('Raja Bernama Seri Mah'raja'), while an extension of the final vowel, 'a', becomes the text for the melisma, which follows. In this final melisma, several commonly used ornaments are also found, including the grace note before the beat, the turn, glissando (or slide), and the use of much thirty-second and sixty-fourth note motion. It is in this passage, too, that the *dalang* takes the liberty to enrich his tonal material by the use of both the natural and sharped forms of the pitches *a* and *c*.

In addition to the vocal ornaments noted in the example from the *bilangan* for Seri Rama, other melodic ornaments are also found in *wayang kulit Siam* melodies and many may be seen in the *serunai* parts throughout the transcriptions of the pieces in Appendix 4. The *serunai* imitates the voice in its use of the glissando (or slide), tremolo (or wide wobble), turn, grace note, and extremely short pitches bounded by rests in the music and likened to the vocal glottal stop. In addition, the *serunai* embellishes its melodic line with the use of the trill, grace notes on the beat, triplet figures, and the staccato articulation of notes (see especially the piece 'Pak Dogol', bars 6–7 and bars 9–10 in Appendix 4).[20]

Within the parameters of the tonal vocabulary, the scales, the melodic ornaments, the melodic contour patterns, and the musical forms, the melodic phrases of the *wayang kulit Siam* music are created to serve as vehicles through which the text of a piece is sung to convey mood or information to the listener, or to relate news among the characters in a story. The *serunai* player uses the musical tools of his tradition to generate long unbroken lines of seemingly free-flowing melody to make a piece 'beautiful', as told by the *wayang kulit* musicians of Kelantan. The fluid, continuous melodies of the *serunai* player, in effect, provide a strong contrast and also an appropriate balance to the otherwise highly percussive nature of the music.

Puppet Movement and the Use of Music

With an insight into how the musical pieces of the *wayang kulit Siam* repertoire are constructed, an understanding of how those pieces are used and what their functions are in an actual performance becomes clearer. During sung pieces, the puppets pose in static scenes, so that as the *dalang* vocalizes specific text, the puppets move only slightly or, indeed, do not move at all. However, as noted earlier in this work, the actual movement of the puppets always requires sound from the orchestra, either as a brief ad lib beating on the instruments (*gertak perkakas*) or as a complete musical piece (*lagu*). At times in a performance when a number of fast puppet movements in quick succession occur, the action on the shadow play screen is accompanied by the simple ad lib beating on the musical instruments. However, in normal circumstances in which any extensive puppet movements occur, a complete musical piece or *lagu* must be played. In this case, the *lagu* sets the mood, gives information or news, or (as purely instrumental music) accompanies specific kinds of puppet movement. The actual manipulation of the puppets is highly stylized and prescribed for the different character-types, and the various kinds of stereotyped movements are accompanied by specific music. Some of the patterns of puppet manipulation are repeated frequently throughout a performance, such as the movements of the parading warriors, or the movements of battle, which are seen again and again, especially as a story draws to a close for the evening. Another type of movement frequently seen is the walking by refined characters. These commonly found types of puppet manipulation all require the accompaniment of specific musical pieces and are illustrated in the discussion below.

One of the first scenes to be performed in every shadow play is the appearance of the wise old sage, the Maharisi. He holds a staff and walks very slowly. When the Maharisi appears, two kinds of puppet manipulation occur: first, a gliding movement for the entrance, exit, or turn of the puppet, and secondly, the walking movement of the puppet. The entrance, exit, or turn movement is accompanied by music referred to as 'Penaik Geduk' [Entrance of Geduk] and, as shown at the beginning of the musical transcription of the piece 'Maharisi' in Appendix 4, the puppet movements are accompanied by specific time-marking patterns played on the percussion idiophones and by rhythmic patterns played on the *gedumbak, gendang,* and *geduk.*

The 'Penaik Geduk' section of the piece features a dotted rhythmic figure and a drum roll played on the stick-hit *geduk.* The entrance movement is first executed at a slow pace with the puppet at a considerable distance from the screen, giving a blurred shadow effect. As the puppet gradually moves towards mid-screen, the slow entrance movement is made in a slight arc shape, accompanied by the dotted rhythm (Figure 1). By the time the puppet is fully on screen, giving a distinct shadow effect, the *geduk* player begins a drum roll which gradually decreases in volume and fades away.

A puppet exit is made in a similar fashion accompanied by the dotted rhythm as the shadow of the puppet becomes blurred and disappears off screen. These movements and their accompanying music are shown in Figure 1, a and b.

As the *geduk* drum roll fades away, the *gedumbak* and *gendang* begin another rhythmic pattern which accompanies the actual movement of walking. The Maharisi is an elderly character and his movements, being slow and deliberate, require a slow tempo in the musical accompaniment. The initial step in the walking movement occurs within the time span of 2 beats. The 2-beat unit is manifested musically as a weak–strong stress pattern played on the *canang* and *kesi* idiophones (see the puppet movement and music in Figure 1(c)). The puppet moves slightly upward, in a rising arc-shaped pattern, on the second half of the first beat, and the movement continues downward and back on the second beat. The walking movement is continued by another upward movement (accompanied by the same rhythmic pattern of the *kesi*) followed by a substantial downward and forward movement, again within the duration of a 2-beat unit. These two steps, backward and forward, are repeated as the puppet moves across the screen. In addition, the rhythmic patterns played on the *gedumbak* and *gendang* take form in 4-beat units and accompany a complete backward and forward step of the puppet.

The action of warriors appearing and parading across the screen is found in many *wayang kulit* stories, and in the *wayang kulit Siam* this action is always accompanied by the piece entitled 'Hulubalang' (a version of the piece is notated in Appendix 4). The piece is cued by the *dalang* who narrates a passage of text stating the characters (usually by name) and their purpose for appearing. His statement is concluded by the nonsense syllables 'ha chap' along with a loud strike on the *pemetik* (Plate 47) at his right knee which cues the musicians to begin the piece 'Hulubalang'. After a very short musical introduction, the main section of the piece commences (that is, the first of many repeated 32-beat gong units begins). The warrior or warriors normally appear on the screen one at a time, and initially parade back and forth across the screen before they are set into the banana tree-trunk to hold them upright at the screen. A given warrior puppet appears accompanied by the sound

FIGURE 1
The Entrance, Exit, Walking Pattern, and Musical Accompaniment
in 'Maharisi'

(a) Entrance   (The screen shown on a vertical plane)

(b) Exit

(c) Walking movement

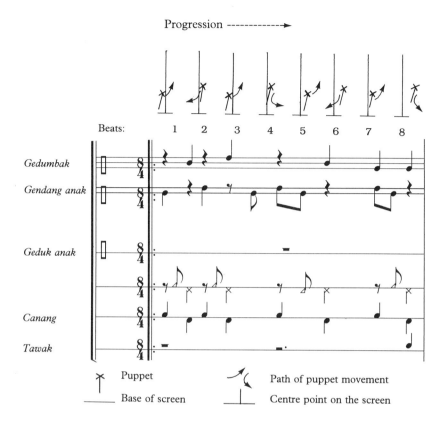

of the lowest-pitched gong in the orchestra (the *tetawak ibu*) and parades across the screen in a set series of movements, reaching the far side of the screen and turning around (usually off screen) simultaneously with the next successive low gong tone in the music. Thus, the puppet parades across the screen in the time taken to complete one 32-beat gong unit in the music.

The drum rhythmic pattern for 'Hulubalang' is also an important factor in accompanying the parading movement. As shown in Appendix 4 ('Hulubalang'), the main rhythmic pattern played on the *gedumbak* is 32 beats in length and may be divided into two contrasting sections. The first section is 16 beats long and consists of specific timbres played on every other beat, punctuated by a musical rest as shown in Figure 2. The tempo of the music and puppet movement is moderate, and one complete 'step' in the actual parading movement occurs in three-dimensional space, the puppet moving to the left and right (or, backward and forward), towards and away from the screen, and upward and downward in a slight arc-shaped pattern. As illustrated in Figure 2(a), a 'step' consists of movement away from the screen on a musical rest (beat 1 of the *gendang*) and movement towards the screen and slightly left (or backward) simultaneously with the *gendang* timbre (beat 2).

FIGURE 2

The Puppet Movement and Music in 'Hulubalang'

(a) Parading 'steps'

(Screen segments, showing centre screen)

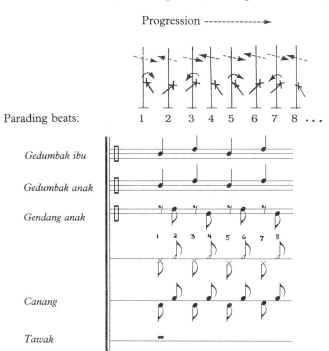

(b) Circular movement at mid-screen

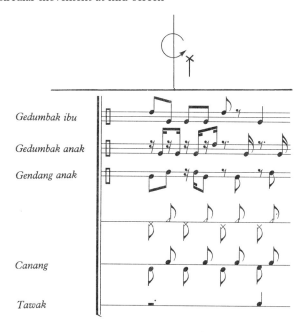

(c) Exit (gliding movement)

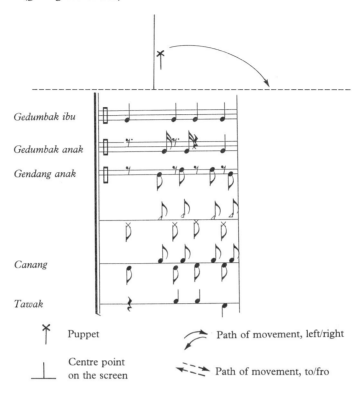

The next parading 'step' takes place as the puppet moves slightly away from the screen again on a rest (beat 3) and then towards the screen and right (or forward) on the next *gendang* timbre (beat 4). These 4 beats are repeated a number of times as the puppet proceeds across the screen (from left to right, for example), arriving at mid-screen on beat 16 of the music. The musical accompaniment up to this point also involves pitch, for it is the two pitches of the small *canang*—the high pitch and the low pitch—which correspond to the puppet movement away from the screen and towards the screen.

The second section of the *gedumbak* pattern in 'Hulubalang' is also 16 beats long, with drum timbres occurring on nearly all beats of the first half of this section (beats 17–24). As shown in Figure 2(b) (circular movement), the drum pattern accompanies the puppet in a small circular movement just at mid-screen, the circle completed with the sounding of the high-pitched gong tone on beat 24. Finally, the last section of the drum pattern (beats 25–32) and the parading 'steps' of the puppet are very similar to the first section in music and puppet movement (Figure 2(a), beats 1–8). The puppet makes its way off screen to the right of the *dalang*'s sitting position at mid-screen (or, if the puppet begins its parading from the right, it exits to the left of the *dalang*). An alternative to the parading 'steps' on beats 25–32 is a smooth gliding movement off screen as shown in Figure 2(c).

Another type of action commonly used in the *wayang kulit* is that of a battle scene in which the puppets are manipulated on many planes parallel as well as oblique to the screen. The puppets move rapidly up and down, left and right, and in a clashing criss-cross fashion as illustrated in Figure 3. The placement of the puppet at the screen and the gliding movements on the screen are characteristic of the action of battle. As the battle ensues, the puppets chase one another across the screen, sometimes making several passes left and then right. Next, the *dalang* holds the puppets facing each other at mid-screen in a brief pause before the attack, and finally he moves the puppets quickly back and forth past one another in criss-cross fashion indicating the confrontation of battle, first to the left, then to the right of the lamp at mid-screen. Sometimes the puppets actually clash heads together in the space parallel to the screen and in front of the lamp. These series of movements may be repeated any number of times during the course of the battle.

The music which accompanies this battle scene is always the *lagu* 'Perang' (notated in Appendix 4). The *dalang* cues this piece to begin by, again, making a statement telling of the imminent battle, uttering the nonsense syllable 'hei', and giving a loud clap on the *pemetik* at his knee. The music begins with a brief introduction indicated by the loud high timbre on the *gedumbak* which is then followed by a loud, low, resonant timbre played on every beat of the drumming pattern. The two stick-hit *geduk* provide the dynamic drumming pattern for this piece consisting of

FIGURE 3
The Music and Puppet Movement in 'Perang'

(Screen on a vertical plane as seen by the *dalang*)

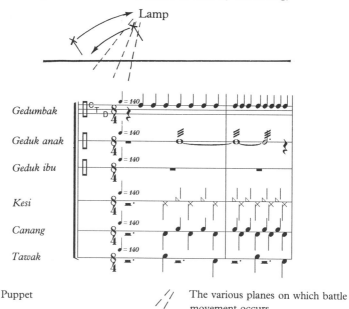

Puppet

Path of movement

The various planes on which battle movement occurs

many drum rolls, triplet figures, and syncopated patterns as shown in the transcription in Appendix 4. The gong unit in the piece 'Perang' is 8 beats in length with the low-pitched gong tone always present on beat 8. As the gong unit is repeated over and over, the *geduk* and *gedumbak* drummers play their given rhythmic patterns, with high, sharp timbres occurring during the times of chase, the pause at the screen, and the clashing of the puppets' heads. Then the drummers change to the loud, low drum timbres which are played during the times of the criss-cross movement of the puppets signalling the confrontation of battle. In this scene, then, the puppets' movements do not necessarily follow the specific gong tones and drum timbres of the time-marking units and rhythmic patterns, as in the piece 'Hulubalang'. The puppet movement is usually very fast as is the tempo of the music.

In some shadow play stories, mythical creatures, birds, and sometimes even demigods descend from the heavens to take part in events alongside earthbound creatures. It is only in these instances that the upper part of the screen is ever used in a shadow play performance. A clear example can be found in the 'Dalang Muda' prologue when the *dewa panah* descend to the stage to battle, and at this time the puppet movement begins not at the far left or right of the normal level of the lamp, but instead far above and directly in line with the lamp.

The two demigods' descent is musically conveyed by the *geduk anak* and *ibu* as shown in Figure 4. The piece known as 'Dewa Panah Turun' [Demigods with Bows and Arrows Descend] is cast in a *gongan* identical to that of the *lagu* 'Perang', the battle piece. Within this 8-beat temporal unit marked by the gongs and cymbals, the *gedumbak* play the low-timbre mnemonic 'dong' on each even-numbered beat in the gong unit. Simultaneously, the two *geduk* alternate in a rhythmic pattern of two drum strokes to the beat. The high timbres of the *geduk anak* occur on the weak beats of the gong unit (beats 1, 3, 5, and 7), while the low timbres of the *geduk ibu* are played on the strong pulses of the colotomic unit (beats 2, 4, 6, and 8).

In the manipulation of the puppets, the *dalang* holds the two demigods (facing each other) high above the lamp with the tips of the puppets' heads barely touching the screen and the base end of the puppet body held oblique to the screen, producing very blurred shadow effects. With the sound of the high-timbre *geduk* and high-pitched *canang* (occurring on the weak beats of the gong unit), the two puppets are moved slightly away from the screen and to the left of the *dalang*. With the drum strokes of the low-timbred *geduk*, *gedumbak*, and the low-pitched *canang* (on the strong beats of the gong unit), the puppets are moved towards the screen and slightly downward, continuing to the *dalang*'s left side. These two basic movements, away from the screen and then downward and towards the screen, are carried out in the time of 2 musical beats. The same pattern of movement away from and towards the screen is continued at the right side of the *dalang* in a 2-beat sequence. As shown in Figure 4, with each successive movement to the right and left of the *dalang*, the bodies of the puppets are gradually lowered until they are nearly parallel to, or almost at, the base of the screen, resulting in distinct shadow forms. The puppet movement of descent consists of basic movements away from and then towards the screen, first to the left of centre screen and then to the right, and simultaneously downward to the base of the screen, closely following the alternating high and low timbres of the *geduk*.

The final type of puppet movement to be noted here is the walking by refined puppet characters. In this type of scene, the puppet makes its appearance at one side of the screen, walks across nearly the entire length of the screen, using stylized 'step' patterns, and makes its exit in a gliding movement off the opposite side of the screen. The puppet may be turned to face the screen and repeat these movements any number of times before it is placed in the banana tree-trunk on screen or taken off screen entirely. The basic movements to be considered here, then, are the stylized 'step' pattern and the gliding movement off screen, both of which are illustrated with the accompanying music in Figure 5.

An example of a musical piece which accompanies the walking movement by refined characters is 'Berjalan' (or alternately, 'Seri Rama

FIGURE 4

The Puppet Movement, Showing Descent from the Heavens,
in 'Dewa Panah Turun'

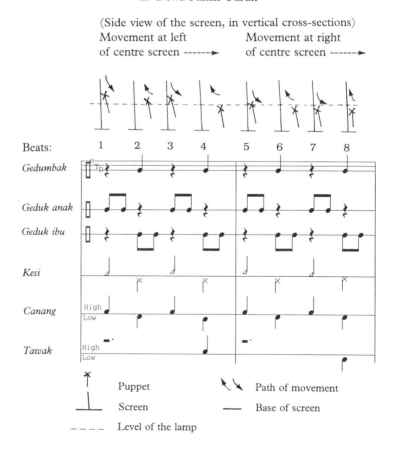

Masuk Istana', or 'Seri Rama Berjalan'). The gong unit, 8-beats in length, once again provides the framework for the organization of musical time and the drum rhythmic patterns in the piece. The two *gendang* play a short 4-beat interlocking rhythmic pattern which is repeated to fill the time of the complete 8-beat gong unit, and specific drum timbres occur on specific beats in the repeated unit as shown in Figure 5. In addition, the high and low pitches of the *canang*, as well as the undamped and damped timbres of the small hand cymbals mark all the beats in the 8-beat gong unit.

FIGURE 5

The Puppet Movement and Music for the Walking Action
by Refined Characters in 'Berjalan'

(a) Walking 'step'

(Screen on a vertical plane as seen by the *dalang*)
Progression of movement ------▶

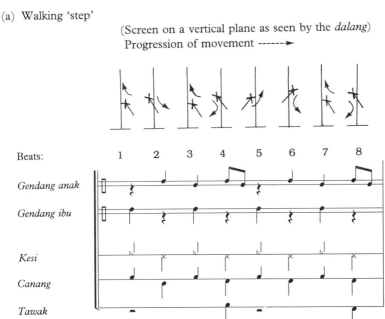

(b) Exit (gliding movement)
    (Aerial view of the screen and performing space)

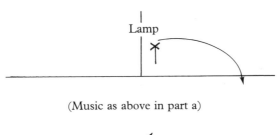

(Music as above in part a)

The stereotyped movement of walking by refined characters occurs in a 2-beat walking 'step', consisting of an upward movement of the puppet (on beat 1) followed by a strong motion downward first to the right (on beat 2). This 2-beat pattern is repeated but with the strong motion downward to the left on beat 4, as shown in Figure 5(a). The puppet continues to be moved in this 4-beat sequence of events until it has walked nearly the complete length of the performing area on the screen. The upward movement in a slight arc-shaped path is always accompanied by a specific timbre played on the large *gendang* and by the high pitch of the *canang*, while the strong downward motion to either the left or right is accompanied by specific timbres played on the small *gendang* as well as by the low pitch of the *canang*. In this way the various puppet movements—upward, downward, to the right, and to the left—correspond directly with the specific musical elements of drum timbres and gong chime pitches.

However, when the puppet leaves the screen, the movement occurs at a rather slow pace and with a gliding motion in a wide elliptical path. The puppet's arm is extended and the shadow effect is at first clear and distinct. But as the puppet is taken further from the screen (in its exiting path), the shadow becomes blurred and slowly fades away. The path of movement is shown in Figure 5(b). The pace of the puppet movement does not correspond directly with the rhythm of the musical accompaniment, and only the low gong tone of the large hanging gong in the orchestra signals the disappearance of the puppet from the screen. This type of scene, the walking by refined characters, is highly intense in its dramatic effect and, along with the other types of puppet movement, illustrates the great variety of stylized puppet movements and music used by the *dalang* of the *wayang kulit Siam*.

1. Judith Becker, 'Toward a Theory of the Derivation of Central Javanese Gamelan Gongan', in *The Traditional Music in Modern Java*, Honolulu: University of Hawaii Press, 1980, Appendix IV.

2. See also Judith Becker, 'Time and Tune in Java', in A. Yengoyan and A. L. Becker (eds.), *The Imagination of Reality: Essays in Southeast Asian Coherence Systems*, Norwood, NJ: Ablex Publishing Co., 1979, pp. 204–8.

3. Judith Becker, in 'Central Javanese Gamelan Gongan', notes the occurrence of the processes of expansion and contraction of the gong unit as part of the concept of *irama* in the music of the Central Javanese gamelan.

4. Ibid. The idea of expansion of the gong unit and the increase of the time interval between beats is compared by Judith Becker to a visual image of dots drawn on a balloon. When the balloon is blown up, the distance between the dots increases, thus allowing for the insertion of more dots. Likewise, when the gong unit expands, the time interval between main pulses becomes greater allowing for the insertion of more beats.

5. An analysis of the piece 'Sedayung Pak Yong' is given in Patricia Matusky, 'Music of the Mak Yong Theater of Malaysia: A Fusion of Southeast Asian Malay and Middle Eastern Islamic Elements', in Ellen Leichtman (ed.), *To the Four Corners*, Harmonie Park Press, in press.

6. Judith Becker, 'The Percussive Patterns in the Music of Mainland Southeast Asia', *Ethnomusicology*, 12, 2 (1968): 173–91.

7. Ibid.

8. Three additional 16-beat formal schemes occur in the *gedumbak* repertoire: *a,a,a,b*, *a,b,b,b*, and *a,b,c,b*. These forms are rarely found and represent atypical patterning in the *gedumbak* drumming style.

9. See the complete notation and discussion of the piece 'Maharaja Rawana' in Patricia Matusky, *Music in the Malay Shadow Puppet Theater*, Vols. I–II, Ann Arbor: University Microfilms, 1980.

10. The complete piece, 'Seri Rama Keluar', is notated and discussed in detail in Matusky, *Music in the Malay Shadow Puppet Theater*.

11. The interlocking style of drumming on the *gedumbak* and *gendang anak* is also found in the pieces entitled 'Hulubalang Menyembah', 'Dewa Keluar', 'Dewa Berjalan', 'Maharaja Rawana', 'Pari', and 'Peran Hutan', which are notated and discussed in Matusky, *Music in the Malay Shadow Puppet Theater*.

12. In his work on the Javanese drumming repertoire, 'Drumming in the Context of Javanese Gamelan' (MA thesis, University of California, Los Angeles, 1967), Harja Susilo defines the principle of motivic progression for the formal scheme *a, a, a, b* as 'antecedent–consequent'.

13. Both pieces are notated and analysed in detail in Matusky, *Music in the Malay Shadow Puppet Theater*.

14. A transcription of the piece can be found in Matusky, *Music in the Malay Shadow Puppet Theater*, pp. 557–64.

15. Transcriptions of these pieces are given in Matusky, *Music in the Malay Shadow Puppet Theater*, pp. 457–79, 488–95, 506–8, 513–15, and 529–30.

16. Ibid., pp. 408–11, 496–500, 509–12, 521–8, 545–56.

17. Albert B. Lord, *The Singer of Tales*, New York: Atheneum, 1973.

18. The use of a partly sung, partly spoken passage intoned on a single pitch is shown in the piece 'Menyembah', notated in Appendix 4.

19. A complete, transcribed version of this piece may be found in Matusky, *Music in the Malay Shadow Puppet Theater*, pp. 412–18.

20. The melodic ornaments used in the melodies of the *wayang kulit* repertoire are also found in other traditional Malay folk theatricals of the north-east region of the Malay Peninsula such as the *mak yong* dance-drama and the *main puteri* healing ritual. The *mak yong* vocal style is discussed in William P. Malm, 'Music in Kelantan, Malaysia and Some of Its Cultural Implications', in *Studies in Malaysian Oral and Musical Traditions*, Michigan Papers on South and Southeast Asia, No. 8, Ann Arbor: University of Michigan Press, 1974, and in Matusky, 'Music of the Mak Yong Theater of Malaysia'.

Epilogue

THE foregoing discussion has encompassed a description and analysis of the many facets of the dominant type of Malay shadow puppet play in Malaysia, the *wayang kulit Siam*. Although no written records survive, it is assumed that in the north Malaysian states the tradition of shadow puppet theatre is very old, probably several centuries old. It has emerged as village folk theatre (in the form known as the *wayang kulit Siam*), as well as a palace-supported tradition (the *wayang kulit Melayu*) which might have been, at one time, more closely tied to a classical art form. The court patronage for the *wayang kulit Melayu* has ceased since Malayan independence or thereabouts and the court shadow play has, for all practical purposes, become extinct.

The *wayang kulit Siam* folk form, on the other hand, thrived at one time in the Malay villages and it is still performed in the northern rural regions where a distinctive Malay style of puppet design, dramatic presentation, and music developed. The music, in particular, exhibits an interesting blend of stylistic elements from both the mainland and island areas of South-East Asia. The instrumentation of the orchestra in itself reflects this fusion or mixture of diverse musical elements from the South-East Asian world. The use of the *gedumbak*, *geduk*, and *kesi* (and the types of rhythmic patterns played on them) is strongly tied to the mainland regions, particularly to the Thai *pi phat* and folk *manora* ensembles of southern Thailand in which these same drums and cymbals are found. The double-headed *gendang* with its braced heads and Y-shaped rattan laces, on the other hand, is found throughout the archipelago and is distinctly a part of the island musical traditions. Although knobbed gongs of all sizes are ubiquitous in South-East Asia, the place of origin of the knobbed, bronze gong is acknowledged to be the Malay world of island South-East Asia. The *serunai*, too, is related to similar reed pipes in the island regions which ultimately may find their origins in the Middle Eastern Islamic culture which had taken root in island South-East Asia since at least the twelfth century AD.

Even stronger ties between island South-East Asian music and the Malaysian shadow play music tradition are found within the parameters of the music system. The use of a cyclical time unit (the *gongan*) marked by a knobbed gong (or gongs) as the basis of musical form and the organization of musical time is probably one of the strongest factors linking the Malay shadow play music to that of the South-East Asian islands, particularly to Java and Bali. The repeated temporal units of the *gongan* in the music of the *wayang kulit Siam* find their parallel in the temporal/melodic cycles in Javanese and Balinese gamelan music. All of these musical traditions are governed by similar underlying principles of time organization and musical structure.

Another strong link between the music of the Malay shadow play and the music of island South-East Asia is the use of an interlocking (or shared) performance technique, particularly with regard to the *gendang* drumming, but also found in the combination of the *gedumbak* and *gendang* interlocking rhythmic patterns. The extremely sophisticated interlocking style producing complex resultant rhythmic and melodic patterns in Balinese music (especially that of the *gender wayang*, the Balinese ensemble used to accompany the shadow puppet theatre), for example, is paralleled by the *gendang* drumming not only in the music of the Malay shadow play but also in the music of the Malay *mak yong* dance-drama. These close ties between the island music cultures and the present-day Malay music cultures of the north Malaysian states are not surprising if, historically, the cultural (and musical) influences of the island peoples are acknowledged to have travelled northward throughout the archipelago since at least the ancient times of the Srivijaya and Majapahit empires.

On the Peninsula itself, serious interest in the Malay *wayang kulit* from the late 1970s to the 1980s in the non-rural sectors was noted earlier in Chapter 1 and included the establishment of the Kelana–Phoenix Company in Kuala Lumpur, the use of the shadow play technique in the productions of modern Malaysian theatre, and the establishment of an academic programme in traditional theatre at one of the major Malaysian universities incorporating the Malay shadow puppet theatre (the *wayang kulit Siam* type) as part of its course of study. In addition, the old, but renovated, Central Market in the heart of Kuala Lumpur, which has become renowned for its stalls of local contemporary art works, crafts, and foods, also serves as a venue for the staging of traditional arts from the rural or outlying regions of the country. These performances at the Central Market in metropolitan Kuala Lumpur occasionally feature the *wayang kulit*, either from Kedah or Kelantan, and they continue to be well attended.

However, in the early 1990s the Malay *wayang kulit* still exists primarily as a village folk performing art, with a very localized, regional outlook. The *dalang* and musicians of Kelantan and Kedah, as well as those still surviving in Terengganu, look primarily to their rural and local urban environments for an audience and for the support and sanction that audience has always given. The *wayang kulit*, over the years, has been known to be used as a vehicle to attract voters in local political elections. Featuring the clown characters in newly contrived stories, local issues are raised and solutions to problems are put forth, explicating the prevailing views of the various political parties. The by-elections in the state of Kedah made prominent use of the shadow puppet theatre in 1991.[1]

Some shadow play troupes are attempting to make changes in their dramatic repertoire and staging to keep up with the changing times. For example, stories have been shortened to only two hours in length and performed on a platform stage built on the back of a lorry as has occurred in the state of Kedah.[2] Electric lamps and microphones have been in use for years, and the puppet characters have changed in their appearance, exhibiting modern hair-dos and dress. Although the rural audience is still present, it is changing rapidly as noted earlier in this book, and the continued support and interest in the shadow play tradition by this rural audience in Malaysia is questionable, especially in the highly conservative regions of the country. Ironically, it may well happen that the survival and continued development of the Malay shadow play will take place in the metropolitan centres of the country in the years to come.

1. See 'Using Wayang Kulit to Woo Voters', *New Straits Times*, 19 December 1991.

2. Noted in S. Simathurai, 'Wayang Kulit Goes Modern', *New Straits Times*, 16 March 1992, p. 29.

Appendices

APPENDIX 1
Synopsis of the Story 'Kerbau Hamuk'

THE story 'Kerbau Hamuk' ['The Buffalo Which Runs Amok'], as summarized here, was performed by the Tuk Dalang Awang Lah in Kelantan and recorded on videotape by Dr William P. Malm in August 1968.

The story is one of the main episodes from the *Cerita Maharaja Rawana*, the Malay oral version of the *Ramayana* epic, and in its summarized form as given here shows the use of specific musical pieces as they support and enhance the story-line and accompany the movement of the puppets. Although the 'Dalang Muda' prologue was performed during the recording of the story in 1968 by the then *dalang muda*, Hamzah bin Awang Amat, it was performed in its standard form and is not given in the summary below.

Summary of the Narration and Music

NARRATION: The *dalang* introduces the story, telling the audience the story is set in Java. He speaks of the young buffalo, Anak Amuk, and tells us that he has killed his father and has run amok.

PUPPET MOVEMENT & MUSIC: The buffalo enters to the tune of 'Binatang Berjalan'.

NARRATION: Anak Amuk tells us that his fight with his father has only increased his blood-lust, and he sets off to destroy all that falls in his path.

MOVEMENT & MUSIC: The buffalo moves across the screen to the piece 'Binatang Berjalan'.

NARRATION: The buffalo goes berserk and attacks everything in his path.

MOVEMENT & MUSIC: The buffalo moves violently, attacking objects around him to the accompaniment of the piece 'Perang'.

NARRATION: The hills and mountains are inhabited by spirits, and these otherworldly beings ask the buffalo why he is causing such destruction to their homeland. They advise him to attack the anthills instead of the mountains.

MOVEMENT & MUSIC: A slight movement of the puppet signifies the buffalo's dialogue with the white ants, to the accompaniment of 'Binatang Berjalan'. Then, as the buffalo rushes at an anthill and attacks the ants, the orchestra plays 'Perang'.

NARRATION: The white ants protest. They tell the buffalo that they are peaceful beings and have secured a place for their family, but now it is destroyed. The buffalo then tells them again how he fought and killed his father and that his blood-lust has not yet been satisfied. The ants advise him to cross the sea and fight Raja Bali of the land of Pakian, and they jump on his horns (accompanied by the *gertak perkakas*) to direct him on his journey. They all set off.

MOVEMENT & MUSIC: The buffalo moves across the screen as he begins his journey with the ants to the land of Pakian. The orchestra plays 'Binatang Berjalan'.

NARRATION: Anak Amuk leaps into the sea and swims to the shores of Pakian, with the white ants perched atop his horns serving as his guide.

MOVEMENT & MUSIC: The buffalo swims to Pakian, accompanied by 'Perang'.

NARRATION: As they arrive in Pakian, the ants descend from the buffalo's horns and bid him farewell (accompanied by a brief *gertak perkakas*). Then Anak Amuk sets off to Raja Bali's plantation.

MOVEMENT & MUSIC: The buffalo walks to the plantation to the accompaniment of 'Binatang Berjalan'.

NARRATION: The buffalo arrives at the plantation (signified by the appearance of the *pokok beringin* on the screen), and because he is famished, he eats everything in sight.

MOVEMENT & MUSIC: The orchestra plays 'Perang' as the buffalo eats his way through the gardens of the plantation.

NARRATION: Because this happens to be the day for gathering the fruits and vegetables in the garden, the gardeners appear on the screen (the orchestra sounds the *gertak perkakas*).

MOVEMENT & MUSIC: The gardeners set off for the garden as the orchestra plays 'Orang Darat'.

NARRATION: When they reach the garden, the gardeners see the destruction the buffalo has caused. They follow the footprints of the buffalo until they encounter him (to the sound of the *gertak perkakas*). When the gardeners question the buffalo, he repeatedly tells them that he belongs to no one, that he is eating because he is hungry and that he does not care to whom the garden belongs. The gardeners attempt to frighten the buffalo away with threats of imprisonment for what he has done, and in the end the buffalo defiantly attacks the gardeners and they flee.

MOVEMENT & MUSIC: The buffalo rushes at the gardeners who, in turn, run off the screen, to the accompaniment of 'Perang'.

NARRATION: The gardeners set off to inform Raja Bali of the events in the garden.

MOVEMENT & MUSIC: The gardeners move across and off the screen with the piece 'Orang Darat'.

NARRATION: *En route* they meet Bali's younger brother, Sagariwa, and they repeat the entire tale. Sagariwa goes to court to inform his brother of the events.

MOVEMENT & MUSIC: The gardeners leave the screen to the accompaniment of the *gertak perkakas*, and Sagariwa goes to his brother to the accompaniment of 'Hulubalang'.

NARRATION: Sagariwa tells Raja Bali of the events and Bali calls his two sons, Anila and Anggada.

MOVEMENT & MUSIC: The two sons rush in to answer their father's call, accompanied by the *gertak perkakas*, followed by the piece 'Perang'.

NARRATION: The entire tale is told to the sons, and they are ordered to investigate events in the plantation and to capture the buffalo.

MOVEMENT & MUSIC: The sons set off for the plantation to the tune of 'Hulubalang'.

NARRATION: The two sons find the buffalo, and after a short verbal exchange the buffalo attacks them. First, Anggada fights Anak Amuk.

MOVEMENT & MUSIC: The buffalo hurls himself at the two sons, and finally Anggada fights the buffalo, to the accompaniment of 'Perang'.

NARRATION: Anggada tells Anila that the buffalo is very strong and it is not easy to overcome him. Anggada fights with the buffalo again.

MOVEMENT & MUSIC: Anggada and the buffalo fight again to the accompaniment of 'Perang'.

NARRATION: Anggada tells Anila that he cannot defeat the buffalo. Then Anila tries to fight with the buffalo.

MOVEMENT & MUSIC: Anila fights the buffalo, to the tune of 'Perang'.

NARRATION: Unable to defeat Anak Amuk, the two sons decide that they will have to rip off the buffalo's horns in order to win next time. The sons return to their father.

MOVEMENT & MUSIC: The two sons return to their father as the orchestra plays 'Hulubalang'.

NARRATION: They inform Raja Bali of the events and ask for a special knife to kill the buffalo. Instead of granting their request, Raja Bali commands his sons and brother to capture the buffalo and to tie it up. The brother, Sagariwa, is not very enthusiastic, but finally agrees to try.

MOVEMENT & MUSIC: Sagariwa, Anila, and Anggada set off to try to capture the buffalo to the accompaniment of 'Hulubalang'.

NARRATION: Anak Amuk sees the three characters and asks if Sagariwa is the king of Bali. Sagariwa replies, 'No, I am his brother.' The buffalo states that he will see no one but the king who, he has been told, is a truly wise man. Sagariwa replies that he was sent by the king to capture and tie up the wild buffalo. The fight begins again, and seeing that the buffalo cannot be defeated, the sons and Sagariwa return to the palace.

MOVEMENT & MUSIC: The fight ensues; then the sons and brother return to Raja Bali to the accompaniment of 'Perang'.

NARRATION: Sagariwa states they cannot capture the buffalo and suggests that Raja Bali himself go. He agrees.

MOVEMENT & MUSIC: Bali goes to meet the buffalo, accompanied by the piece 'Hulubalang'.

NARRATION: Raja Bali and Anak Amuk meet, and the buffalo tells his story again. They fight.

MOVEMENT & MUSIC: Raja Bali and the buffalo fight as the orchestra plays 'Perang'.

NARRATION: Raja Bali remarks that the buffalo is not an easy opponent. He tries to defeat the animal one more time.

MOVEMENT & MUSIC: They fight again with the piece 'Perang' accompanying the action on the screen.

NARRATION: Raja Bali tells Sagariwa, Anila, and Anggada that he cannot defeat the buffalo, and he has decided he will fight in a cave. He orders Sagariwa to wait outside, and if white blood issues forth (Bali has white blood), they must seal the entrance. But if red blood emerges, it will be the buffalo's and they need take no action.

MOVEMENT & MUSIC: Raja Bali rushes off to fight the buffalo as the piece 'Perang' is played by the orchestra.

NARRATION: Raja Bali challenges Anak Amuk to fight in the cave, and the buffalo agrees.

MOVEMENT & MUSIC: They set off for the cave as the *pokok beringin* appears on the screen (signalling the cave). The piece 'Hulubalang' is played.

NARRATION: The fight begins.

MOVEMENT & MUSIC: Raja Bali and Anak Amuk fight, to the accompaniment of 'Perang'.

NARRATION: Raja Bali doubts that the buffalo's strength is his own, and he suspects that other supernatural beings are helping him. The buffalo says that his strength is his own. In fact, the *dewa empat* (four demigods) are indeed helping Anak Amuk, and entered his hooves at the time he was about to fight his father (the demigods appear on the screen). The *dewa empat* are indignant that the buffalo allows them no credit and they decide to desert him. The narration throughout this scene is punctuated by the *gertak perkakas* rattling of the instruments. The *dewa empat* ascend and disappear.

MOVEMENT & MUSIC: The *dewa empat* leave the screen (the shadows gradually become larger and less distinct, and finally the demigods totally disappear with an ascending motion). The piece played is 'Perang'.

NARRATION: Raja Bali has seen the demigods emerge and he realizes that he can now kill the buffalo. They fight again and Raja Bali kills Anak Amuk.

MOVEMENT & MUSIC: They fight and the buffalo dies, accompanied by the piece 'Perang'.

NARRATION: Sagariwa sees what he takes to be white blood. In fact, it is foam from the buffalo's mouth. He, Anila, and Anggada seal the entrance to the cave.

MOVEMENT & MUSIC: Sagariwa, Anila, and Anggada seal the cave (the *pokok beringin* appears on the screen sealing the cave as the piece 'Perang' is played by the orchestra).

NARRATION: In the cave, Raja Bali has killed the buffalo, and the *dalang* talks about the dangers of pride. Bali then goes to the entrance of the cave.

MOVEMENT & MUSIC: Raja Bali goes to the entrance of the cave, accompanied by the piece 'Hulubalang'.

NARRATION: Raja Bali finds the entrance sealed, and he is at first angry and then sorrowful. He thinks of the errors of kingship and says, 'You want to destroy life and forget the wisdom of your teachers.' The king explains that when he strangled the buffalo, its saliva looked like white blood. Therefore, his brother sealed the cave and now he, too, must die along with the buffalo. He cannot tell night from day. He falls to the floor, weeps, and then faints.

MOVEMENT & MUSIC: Raja Bali falls to the floor, cries, and faints, accompanied by the piece entitled 'Teriak'.

NARRATION: Sagariwa, presuming Bali to be dead, asks Anila and Anggada who should become ruler. They both state that he, Sagariwa, should rule. Sagariwa tells them that one of Bali's wives is, in fact, rightly his, for Bali cheated him out of this bride in the past. Sagariwa asks his nephews to inform Bali's wives of recent events.

MOVEMENT & MUSIC: The three characters return to the palace. The three wives appear on the screen as 'Hulubalang' is played.

NARRATION: The wives talk together of the mad buffalo's attack. Suddenly Anila and Anggada enter.

MOVEMENT & MUSIC: Raja Bali's sons enter to the accompaniment of 'Perang'.

NARRATION: Anila and Anggada inform the wives of current events and of Bali's supposed death, adding that the princesses are now to become the wives of Sagariwa.

MOVEMENT & MUSIC: The wives disappear. Anila and Anggada then go to inform Sagariwa, to the accompaniment of 'Hulubalang'.

NARRATION: Anila and Anggada inform Sagariwa who then presents himself to Raja Bali's wives (the wives reappear).

MOVEMENT & MUSIC: Sagariwa presents himself to the wives, accompanied by the piece 'Hulubalang'.

NARRATION: Sagariwa greets the women, informs them that they are now his wives, and they lie down and sleep together.

MOVEMENT & MUSIC: Sagariwa and the princesses sleep together (their eyes are covered by their arms) as the piece 'Mengulit' is sung.

NARRATION: Meanwhile at the cave, Raja Bali is still unconscious. The *dewa empat*, aware of the buffalo's death, descend into the cave.

MOVEMENT & MUSIC: The spirits appear on the screen to the accompaniment of 'Perang'.

NARRATION: The demigods then give advice to Raja Bali in a dream. Bali should behead the buffalo and hurl the head at the entrance to the cave.

MOVEMENT & MUSIC: The spirits reascend, accompanied by the piece 'Perang'.

NARRATION: Raja Bali awakes; he remembers the advice of the demigods and follows it by cutting off the buffalo's head.

MOVEMENT & MUSIC: Bali awakes and beheads the buffalo, to the accompaniment of 'Perang'.

NARRATION: He then hurls the head at the entrance of the cave.

MOVEMENT & MUSIC: Bali hurls the head at the entrance and the cave is no longer sealed (the buffalo puppet is hurled across the screen and disappears as the piece 'Perang' is played).

NARRATION: The way out is now clear and Raja Bali sets out for home.

MOVEMENT & MUSIC: Bali makes his way back to the palace, to the accompaniment of 'Hulubalang'.

NARRATION: Finding no one outside the palace, he enters.

MOVEMENT & MUSIC: Raja Bali enters the palace accompanied by the piece 'Hulubalang'.

NARRATION: Raja Bali finds Sagariwa sleeping with his (Bali's) wives. He ties the women's hair together and throws Sagariwa out into the jungle.

MOVEMENT & MUSIC: Raja Bali's brother is banished into the jungle, to the accompaniment of 'Perang'.

NARRATION: The women awake and are most distressed; as they see Raja Bali, they try to explain and then beg for forgiveness. Bali beats them.

MOVEMENT & MUSIC: Bali beats his wives, to the accompaniment of 'Perang'.

NARRATION: The princesses sing, begging for forgiveness, accompanied by the piece 'Berkhabar'.

MOVEMENT & MUSIC: The wives leave the screen. Raja Bali remains. The piece 'Berkhabar' is concluded.

[Another piece, 'Hulubalang', is played at this time in the performance because the lamp has gone out and must be re-lit.]

NARRATION: Raja Bali then decides to punish Anila and Anggada. He calls out to them.

MOVEMENT & MUSIC: The two sons Anila and Anggada rush to the scene. The piece 'Perang' is played.

NARRATION: Raja Bali, furious with his sons, rejects their explanation and kicks them.

MOVEMENT & MUSIC: Raja Bali rejects the pleas of his sons as 'Perang' is played by the orchestra.

NARRATION: Raja Bali refuses to pardon his sons and drives them out. Anila and Anggada weep and depart.

MOVEMENT & MUSIC: The two sons leave the screen to the strains of 'Hulubalang'.

NARRATION: The *dalang* states that the story will be continued on the following night.

MUSIC: The piece 'Seri Rama Keluar' is played here as closing music.

APPENDIX 2
The Musical Repertoire of the Kelantanese *Wayang Kulit Siam*

List of Musical Pieces (*Lagu*):

1 'Maharisi' [Maharisi], used for the appearance and walking action of the sage

2 'Dewa Panah Turun' [Demigods with Bows and Arrows Descend]

3 'Dewa Panah Perang' [Demigods with Bows and Arrows Battle]

4 'Hulubalang' [Warriors], used for the parading action of warriors, or 'Dewa Panah Berjalan' [Demigods with Bows and Arrows Walk]

5 'Seri Rama Keluar' [Seri Rama Appears], or 'Seri Rama dengan Gedumbak' [Seri Rama (played on the *gedumbak*)]

6 'Menyembah' [To Pay Homage]

7 'Berkhabar' [To Give News], also known as 'Tanya Khabar' [To Ask for News], or 'Khabar Wayang' [News of the Shadow Play]

8 'Seri Rama Masuk Istana' [Seri Rama Enters the Palace], also known as 'Seri Rama Berjalan' [Seri Rama Walks] or simply 'Berjalan' [Walking], by a refined character

9 'Perang' [To Battle]

10 'Bertabuh' [Beating the Drums]

11 'Pak Dogol' [Pak Dogol], used for the appearance and walking of the character by that name

12 'Dewa Keluar' [Demigods Appear], used for the appearance of all demigods other than the *dewa panah*

13 'Bertukar Dalang' [To Change the Puppeteer], played to signal the departure of the deputy *dalang* and the commencing of the main story by the puppet master

14 'Dewa Berjalan' [Demigods Walk], used for the walking action of the demigods but frequently used as the piece for changing the puppeteer

15 'Binatang Berjalan' [Animals Walk]

16 'Orang Darat' [Country Bumpkins], used for the appearance of the country bumpkins

17 'Main Alun' [To Play as if Echoing], playing in the manner of echoing or reverberating; also known as 'Menggali' [To Dig]

18 'Pari' [Fairies], used for the appearance of fairies

19 'Menghendap' [To Crouch in Ambush]; also known as 'Menghindar' [To Avert Danger] or 'Memburu' [To Hunt]

20 'Peran Hutan' [Jungle Clown], used for the appearance of the character by that name

21 'Maharaja Rawana' [Maharaja Rawana], used for the appearance of the character by that name
22 'Hulubalang Menyembah' [Warriors Pay Homage]
23 'Sang Kaki' [Sang Kaki], used for the appearance of the character by that name
24 'Sedayung' (meaning unknown), used in general when a sung piece is required
25 'Tidur' [To Sleep], also known as 'Mengulit' [To Lull], 'Mandi' [To Bathe], 'Minum' [To Drink], 'Baca Surat' [To Read a Letter], and 'Memetik Bunga' [To Pick Flowers], depending on the situation
26 'Barat Cepat', a travelling piece in a fast tempo
27 'Barat Patah', a travelling piece played with a distinctive drumming pattern considered to be disconnected in style
28 'Barat Anjur' or 'Barat Lambat', a travelling piece in a slow tempo
29 'Menangis' [To Weep]
30 'Khabar dan Dayang' [News of the Maiden]

APPENDIX 3
Summary of the Musical Forms

EACH letter in the 'Cycles' column represents one musical beat. The letter 'd' is one stroke on the *canang anak*, 'D' is one stroke on the *canang ibu*, 'g' is one stroke on the *tawak anak*, and 'G' is one stroke on the *tawak ibu*. When two letters are aligned vertically, they are played simultaneously in the time of one beat.

I. *The Basic Musical Forms*	*Musical Pieces*
8-beat Temporal Cycles	
⎡ d D d D d D d D ⎤ ⎣ **g** **G** ⎦	'Bertabuh', 'Perang', 'Pak Dogol', 'Barat', 'Dewa Keluar', 'Berjalan', 'Dewa Panah Turun', 'Dewa Panah Perang'
⎡ d D d D d D d D ⎤ ⎣ **g** **g** **G** ⎦	Cadential gong unit
16-beat Temporal Cycles	

⎡ d D d D d D d D
                 g
d D d D d D d D ⎤
                G ⎦
	'Maharisi', 'Bertukar Dalang', 'Orang Darat', 'Binatang Berjalan', 'Dewa Berjalan', 'Sang Kaki', 'Peran Hutan', 'Menggali'/'Main Alun', 'Menghendap'/'Menghindar'/'Memburu'

⎡ d D d D d D d D
                g
d D d D d D d D ⎤
  g   **g**   **G** ⎦
	Cadential gong unit

$$
\begin{bmatrix}
\text{d D d D d D d D} \\
\quad\;\; \textbf{g} \qquad\quad \textbf{g} \\
\text{d D d D d D d D} \\
\quad\;\; \textbf{g} \quad \textbf{g} \quad \textbf{G}
\end{bmatrix}
\qquad \text{'Sedayung'}
$$

32-beat Temporal Cycles

$$
\begin{bmatrix}
\text{d D d D d D d D} \\
\text{d D d D d D d D} \\
\qquad\qquad\quad\; \textbf{g} \\
\text{d D d D d D d D} \\
\qquad\qquad\quad\; \textbf{g} \\
\text{d D d D d D d D} \\
\quad\; \textbf{g} \quad \textbf{g} \quad \textbf{G}
\end{bmatrix}
\qquad
\begin{array}{l}\text{'Hulubalang', 'Hulubalang} \\ \text{Menyembah'}\end{array}
$$

$$
\begin{bmatrix}
\text{d D d D d D d D} \\
\text{d D d D d D d D} \\
\qquad\qquad\quad\; \textbf{g}
\end{bmatrix}
\qquad \text{'Seri Rama Keluar'}
$$
$$
\begin{array}{l}
\text{d D d D d D d D} \\
\text{d D d D d D d D} \\
\qquad\qquad\qquad \textbf{G}
\end{array}
$$

$$
\begin{bmatrix}
\text{d D d D d D d D} \\
\qquad\qquad\quad\; \textbf{g} \\
\text{d D d D d D d D} \\
\qquad\qquad\quad\; \textbf{g} \\
\text{d D d D d D d D} \\
\qquad\qquad\quad\; \textbf{g} \\
\text{d D d D d D d D} \\
\quad\; \textbf{g} \quad \textbf{g} \quad \textbf{G}
\end{bmatrix}
\qquad
\begin{array}{l}\text{'Menyembah', 'Saudara', 'Kijang} \\ \text{Mas', all } \textit{lagu menyanyi}\end{array}
$$

II. *The Compound Musical Forms*   *Musical Pieces*

32-beat Temporal Cycles

$$
\begin{bmatrix}
\text{d D d D d D d D} \\
\quad\; \textbf{g} \qquad\quad \textbf{G} \\
\text{d D d D d D d D} \\
\quad\; \textbf{g} \qquad\quad \textbf{G} \\
\text{d D d D d D d D} \\
\quad\; \textbf{g} \qquad\quad \textbf{G} \\
\text{d D d D d D d D} \\
\quad\; \textbf{g} \quad \textbf{g} \quad \textbf{G}
\end{bmatrix}
\qquad
\begin{array}{l}\text{'Tidur', 'Mengulit', 'Mandi',} \\ \text{'Minum', 'Baca Surat', 'Memetik} \\ \text{Bunga'}\end{array}
$$

$$
\left[
\begin{array}{l}
\text{d D d D d D d D} \\
\qquad\qquad\qquad\quad \textbf{g} \\
\\
\text{d D d D d D d D} \\
\qquad\qquad\qquad\quad \textbf{G} \\
\\
\text{d D d D d D d D} \\
\qquad\qquad\qquad\quad \textbf{g} \\
\\
\text{d D d D d D d D} \\
\quad \textbf{g} \qquad\qquad \textbf{G}
\end{array}
\right]
\qquad \text{'Barat Anjur', 'Barat Patah'}
$$

48-beat Temporal Cycles

$$
\left[
\begin{array}{l}
\text{d D d D d D d D} \\
\qquad\qquad\qquad\quad \textbf{g} \\
\\
\text{d D d D d D d D} \\
\qquad\qquad\qquad\quad \textbf{G} \\
\\
\text{d D d D d D d D} \\
\qquad\qquad\qquad\quad \textbf{g} \\
\\
\text{d D d D d D d D} \\
\qquad\qquad\qquad\quad \textbf{G} \\
\\
\text{d D d D d D d D} \\
\qquad\qquad\qquad\quad \textbf{g} \\
\\
\text{d D d D d D d D} \\
\quad \textbf{g} \quad\;\; \textbf{g} \quad\;\; \textbf{G}
\end{array}
\right]
\qquad
\begin{array}{l}
\text{'Berkhabar', 'Khabar Wayang',} \\
\text{'Tanya Khabar'}
\end{array}
$$

$$
\left[
\begin{array}{l}
\text{d D d D d D d D} \\
\\
\text{d D d D d D d D} \\
\qquad\qquad\qquad\quad \textbf{g} \\
\\
\text{d D d D d D d D} \\
\qquad\qquad\qquad\quad \textbf{g} \\
\\
\text{d D d D d D d D} \\
\quad \textbf{g} \quad\;\; \textbf{g} \quad\;\; \textbf{G} \\
\\
\text{d D d D d D d D} \\
\qquad\qquad\qquad\quad \textbf{g} \\
\\
\text{d D d D d D d D} \\
\quad \textbf{g} \quad\;\; \textbf{g} \quad\;\; \textbf{G}
\end{array}
\right]
\qquad \text{'Menangis', 'Maharaja Rawana'}
$$

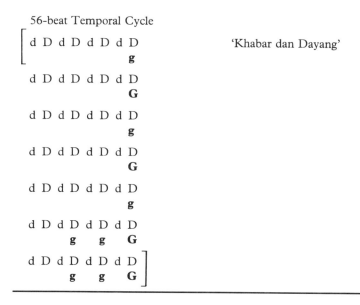

56-beat Temporal Cycle

'Khabar dan Dayang'

APPENDIX 4
Transcriptions of Select *Wayang Kulit Siam* Musical Pieces

Notes on the Transcriptions

A modified staff notation has been used to transcribe the musical pieces in score. The top staff is reserved for instrumental or vocal melody. The drums (*gedumbak, geduk,* and *gendang*) are placed on the middle staves, while the gong and cymbal parts are written on the lower staves. The bottom staff is used for the *geduk* drum pattern which signals the cadence at the end of the piece.

The musical pieces of the Kelantanese *wayang kulit* repertoire have been transcribed from field recordings made by the author from 1976 to 1978, as well as from field notes taken by the author during private instruction in 1976. In some cases, a piece is written in abbreviated form with continuation or extension of the musical material indicated in the score.

The gong unit usually dictates the placement of the bar line by a solid vertical bar appearing at the end of each gong unit. However, in the case of very long gong units (32 beats or more), a convenient number of beats has been selected (usually following the structure of the drum rhythmic patterns in a given piece) to represent one bar in the music. This deviation in the notation of the gong unit is used here mainly for ease in reading the score.

The melodic parts, either vocal or instrumental, appear on the 5-line staff using standard notation along with certain supplementary symbols. The added symbols are shown in the list which follows below. The change of vocal and instrumental parts is indicated above the melody staff.

The percussive rhythmic patterns played on the drums are written on staff lines which correspond to the specific mnemonic sounds produced on the individual instruments. The *gedumbak anak* and *ibu* (small and large sizes), for example, each produce four basic timbres which are written on specific lines of the staff. The mnemonic sound 'chap' is abbreviated as 'C', the mnemonic 'dong' is 'D', the mnemonic 'duh' is written as 'd', and the mnemonic 'ting' is abbreviated as 'T' for the *gedumbak*. Each abbreviation is placed at the beginning of a specific line of the drum staff. The actual rhythmic patterns are then written in standard rhythmic notation.

The *gendang anak* produces two timbres. The mnemonic 'chap' is written as 'c' and the mnemonic 'ting' is written as 't' on the *gendang anak* staff. The *gendang ibu* produces two timbres of sound vocalized as 'chap' (or 'pak') and 'duh'. Consequently, on the staff for the *gendang ibu* the mnemonic 'chap' is written as 'c' and the mnemonic 'duh' is abbreviated as 'd'.

No standard mnemonic system is used for the rhythmic patterns played on the two *geduk*. Both the *geduk anak* and *ibu* are written on separate staves and their respective rhythmic patterns are written in standard notation.

The pair of small pot-shaped, knobbed gongs called *canang* provides two pitches in high register. The two pitches are often found at an interval of approximately one whole step apart. The high pitch is written in standard notation above the staff line with stem up representing a stroke on the gong with the left hand. The low-pitched *canang* is also written in standard notation, but is found below the staff line with stem down representing a stroke with the right hand. Although the tuning of the two small gongs is not standard, an effort is made to tune the *canang ibu* compatibly with the large hanging gong of high pitch (called the *tawak anak*).

The pair of large hanging gongs called *tetawak* or *tawak* provides two pitches in low register. The pitches are often heard at an interval of about three or four semitones apart (approximating a minor or major third). The high pitch, referred to as *anak*, is written above the *tawak* single-line staff, while the low pitch, called *ibu*, is written below the staff. The time of impact on the knob of the gong is indicated by the placement of the symbol in the score, but no durational value is given to either *tawak* note. Like the *canang*, the tuning of the large hanging gongs is not standard from one set to another.

The small hand cymbals called *kesi* produce two timbres, damped and undamped. The damped timbre is a non-ringing sound (often vocalized as 'chap') indicated by the special note shape (listed in the following table of supplementary symbols) which is written below the single-line staff for the *kesi*. The undamped timbre is a sonorous, ringing sound (often vocalized as 'ching') written using a special shaped note above the staff line.

Supplementary Notation Symbols

Symbol	Meaning
	A pitch slightly higher than written.
	A pitch slightly lower than written.
	A slide (glissando) from one pitch to another.
	A slide occurring for the duration of 2 or more beats as indicated by the vertical bars above the symbol.

Symbol	Meaning
	Grace note (notes) occurring before the downbeat.
	Trill, a rapid alternation of the basic pitch to the pitch above.
	Tie, when written between two notes of the same pitch. Slur, when written between two notes of different pitch.
	Staccato.
	Accented note.
	A combination of speech and song showing inflection and tessitura, but not necessarily exact pitch.
	Glottal stop written in the text and shown in the musical notation as a rest of specific time value.
	A tremolo or wobble; an alternation of two pitches which may be slow or fast; pitch and rhythm are often indeterminant.
and so on . . .	Continuation of musical material.
	Mnemonic 'ting'.
	Mnemonic 'chap'.
	Mnemonic 'duh'.
	Mnemonic 'dong'.
	Undamped *kesi* ('ching').
	Damped *kesi* ('chap').

TRANSCRIPTION 1
'Pak Dogol'*

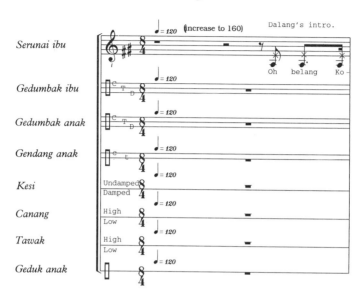

*Scale

Serunai ibu

Gedumbak ibu

Gedumbak anak

Gendang anak

Kesi

Canang

Tawak

Geduk anak

Serunai ibu

Gedumbak ibu

Gedumbak anak

Gendang anak

Kesi

Canang

Tawak

Geduk anak

Serunai ibu

Gedumbak ibu

Gedumbak anak

Gendang anak

Kesi

Canang

Tawak

Geduk anak

Serunai ibu

Gedumbak ibu

Gedumbak anak

Gendang anak

Kesi

Canang

Tawak

Geduk anak

TRANSCRIPTION 2
'Binatang Berjalan'*

Serunai ibu

Gedumbak ibu

Gedumbak anak

Gendang anak

Kesi

Canang

Tawak

Geduk anak

Scale

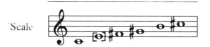

TRANSCRIPTION 3
'Hulubalang'*

TRANSCRIPTION 4
'Berjalan'*

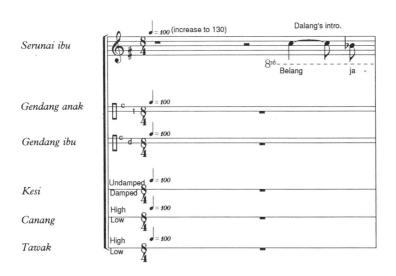

'Scale

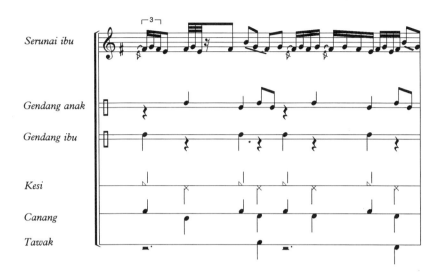

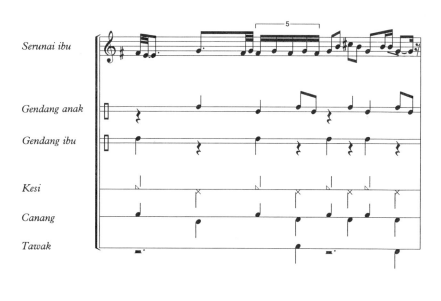

TRANSCRIPTION 5
'Menyembah'*
(Introduction and one *gongan*)

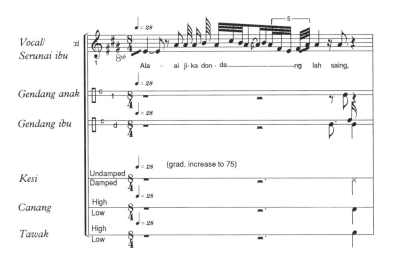

*Scale

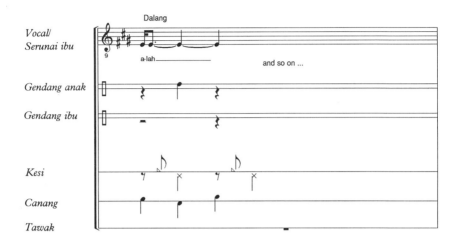

TRANSCRIPTION 6
'Perang'*

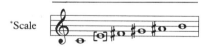
*Scale

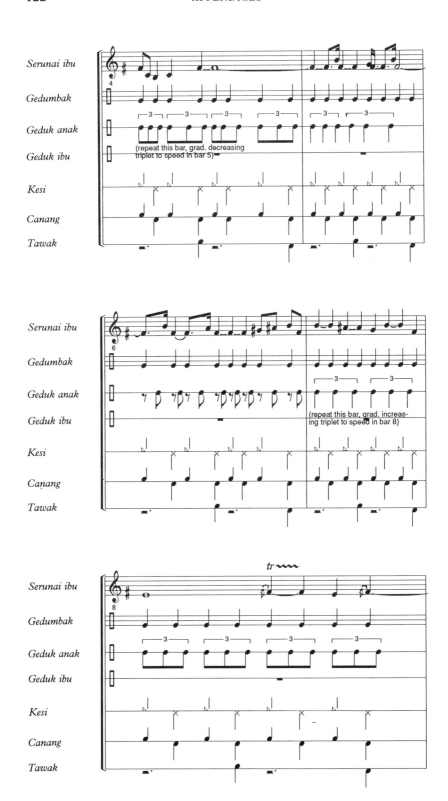

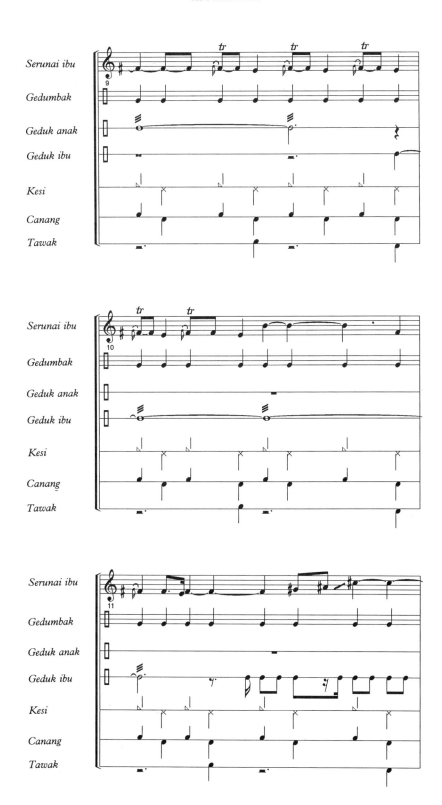

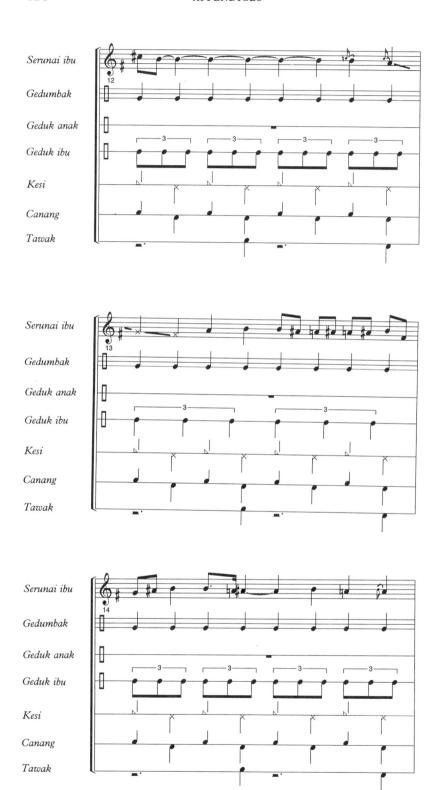

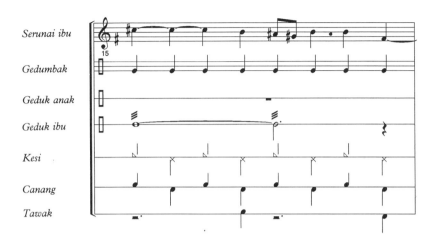

TRANSCRIPTION 7
'Orang Darat'*

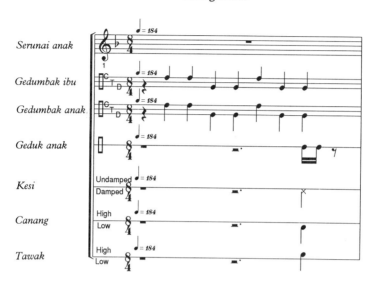

*Scale

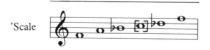

Serunai anak

Gedumbak ibu

Gedumbak anak

Geduk anak

Kesi

Canang

Tawak

TRANSCRIPTION 8
'Maharisi'*

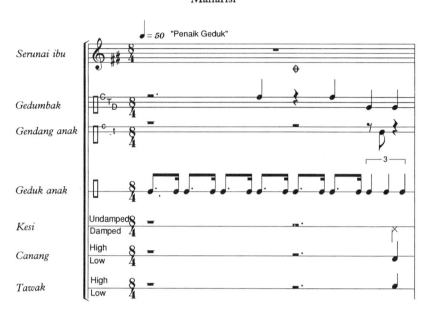

*Scale

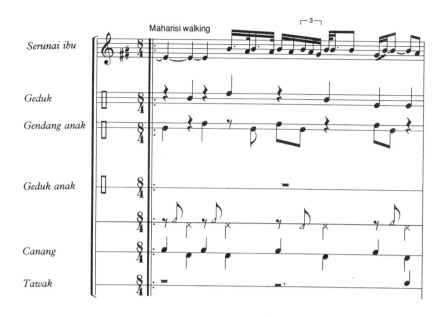

Glossary

adat	customary Malay law governing the family unit with regard to life-cycle events, social life, and behaviour
adik	younger brother, sister
anak	child; in musical terminology, the higher of two pitches, or the smaller of two instruments of the same kind
anjur	slow tempo in music
atap	thatched reeds
ayak-ayak	a musical form used in the Javanese *wayang kulit purwa*
balai	receiving hall of the palace
bangsawan	Malay opera
bapa	father
batang	stick
batang pisang	banana tree-trunk
beca	pedicab
berjamu	feasting of the spirits, a high ritual performance of the *wayang kulit Siam*
bilangan	formal descriptive text in rhythmic prose
binatang	animal
bomoh	spirit medium, shaman
bonang	gong chime found in the Javanese gamelan
boria	popular theatre (comprising dance, song, and sketch) originating from Penang
buka panggung	the ceremony for the official opening of a shadow play stage
bunga	flower; musical embellishment manifested as pitch or drum timbre
canang	small gong chime (usually two gongs set in a wooden rack)
caping	lip disc on the *serunai*
cerita	story
cerita bunga	literally, flower stories; lesser known stories of the *wayang kulit Siam*
cerita daun	literally, leaf stories; like *cerita bunga*, lesser known stories of the *wayang kulit Siam*
cerita ranting	literally, branch stories; more frequently told stories of the *wayang kulit Siam*
'chap'	mnemonic timbre produced on a drum
Chawa	the Thai name for Java

dalang	puppeteer in the shadow puppet theatre
'Dalang Muda'	the prologue to the *wayang kulit Siam*, also referred to as the 'Tuk Dalang Muda', named after the deputy puppeteer (the *dalang muda*) who performs it
dalang tiru	*dalang* by imitation
dayang	maiden
demung	the large-sized *sarun* in the Javanese gamelan
dewa	demigod
dewa laki-laki	male godling; the *dewa panah* with unrefined facial traits, representing the forces of evil
dewa panah	demigod carrying a bow and arrow or a small sword
dewa perempuan	female godling; the *dewa panah* with refined facial traits, representing the forces of good
'ding-dong'	vocalization of the high and low pitches, respectively, on the *canang*; vocal representation of the weak and strong stresses, respectively, in the gong unit
'dong'	mnemonic timbre produced on a drum
'duh'	mnemonic timbre produced on a drum
gambang	wooden xylophone in the Javanese gamelan
gamelan	ensemble of Central Java, made up primarily of bronze knobbed gongs and metallophones, but also including xylophones, bowed lutes, flutes, and drums
geduk	short, double-headed barrel drum hit with sticks in the *wayang kulit Siam* orchestra
gedumbak	single-headed goblet-shaped drum hit with the hands in the *wayang kulit Siam* orchestra
gendang	large, elongated double-headed drum hit with the hands in the *wayang kulit Siam* orchestra
gendang silat	music which accompanies the *silat* (Malay art of self-defence)
gender	metallophone with tube resonators in the Javanese gamelan
gertak perkakas	ad lib beating on the musical instruments
gong	bronze, knobbed percussion idiophone struck with a padded beater
gong agung	the largest and lowest-pitched gong in the Javanese gamelan
gong suwukan	the second largest and lowest-pitched gong in the Javanese gamelan
gongan	a cyclical time unit made up of a specific number of beats and marked on the last beat by a stroke on the gong
gunungan	mountain, the tree of life puppet in the Javanese shadow play; also called the *kayon*
halus	refined
hulubalang	warrior
ibu	mother; in musical terminology, the lower of two pitches, or the larger of two instruments of the same kind
joget	popular social dance music
joget gamelan	the court music and dance tradition of Pahang and Terengganu
kasar	coarse, vulgar

kayon	tree of life puppet in the Javanese shadow play; also called the *gunungan*
kecopong	bell-shaped lower end of the *serunai*
kelir	white cloth screen of the shadow play stage
kempul	a set of hanging knobbed gongs in the Javanese gamelan
kenduri	feast
kenong	a set of large, knobbed pot-shaped gongs in the Javanese gamelan
kesi	small hand cymbals
ketuk	a small knobbed pot-shaped gong in the Javanese gamelan
lagu	musical piece or scene in the shadow play
main puteri	exorcism ritual performed by a *bomoh* (shaman) to the accompaniment of music
mali	tubular reed carrier on the *serunai*
mak yong	the Malay dance-drama
mandi	to bathe
manora	the southern Thai dance-drama
membaca surat	to read a letter
memburu	to hunt
memetik bunga	to pick a flower
menangis	to cry
menggali	to dig
menghendap	to crouch, stalk
menghindar	to avoid danger
menyanyi	to sing
menyemah	a type of *berjamu* ceremony for the adjustment of 'winds' or emotions
minum	to drink
mong	a medium-sized pot-shaped knobbed gong
nang sbek	the shadow puppet theatre of Cambodia using large non-articulated leather puppets and scenes
nang talung	the shadow puppet theatre of southern Thailand using small, articulated leather puppets
nang yai	the shadow puppet theatre of Thailand using large, non-articulated leather puppets and scenes
orang darat	unsophisticated country folk
padi	rice, paddy
'pak'	mnemonic timbre produced on a drum
pandai	skilled
panggung	stage for a theatrical performance
pangkal	bell-shaped lower end of the *serunai*
panjak	troupe of musicians
pari	spirit-fairies
patah	broken, disconnected
patung	puppet
pelepas niat	release from a vow; a type of *berjamu* for this purpose
pelimau	the ritual bathing with lime water; a type of *berjamu* for the ritual bathing of a student
pelita	lamp used as the source of light for the shadow play
pembukaan	the ceremony for the official opening of a shadow play stage

pemetik	wooden clapper, a signalling device used in the *wayang kulit Siam* shadow play
perang	to battle
pipit	reed of the *serunai*
pokok beringin	banyan tree; the tree of life puppet in the *wayang kulit Siam*
pokok lontar	palmyra palm
raksaksa	ogre
rebab	two-stringed bowed instrument in the *wayang kulit Melayu* orchestra
sajian	food offerings for a ceremony
sampak	a musical form used in the Javanese *wayang kulit purwa*
sarun	metallophone with trough resonator in the Javanese gamelan
sembah	to pay obeisance
serunai	quadruple-reed aerophone (shawm)
slenthem	a large-size metallophone with tube resonators found in the Javanese gamelan
srepegan	a musical form used in the Javanese *wayang kulit purwa*
suwukan	a hanging bronze knobbed gong in the Javanese gamelan
teriak	to cry
tetawak/tawak	a large, bronze knobbed gong
tidur	to sleep
'ting'	mnemonic timbre produced on a drum
'Tuk Dalang Muda'	the prologue to the *wayang kulit Siam* shadow play; also known simply as 'Dalang Muda'
ucap	formal descriptive text in rhythmic prose
wayang Kelantan	alternate name sometimes used for the *wayang kulit Siam*
wayang kulit Gedek	a Malay form of shadow puppet theatre, closely related to the Thai *nang talung* and found in the north-west Malaysian states
wayang kulit Jawa	the Javanese shadow puppet theatre (*wayang kulit purwa*) performed in the southern Malaysian state of Johor and formerly in Selangor; also an alternate name for the *wayang kulit Melayu*
wayang kulit Melayu	a Malay form of shadow puppet theatre, heavily influenced by the Javanese *wayang kulit purwa* and found in the northern Malaysian states, but nearly extinct today
wayang kulit Siam	the pre-eminent form of Malay shadow puppet theatre using small articulated leather puppets, and found in the northern Malaysian states
wayang kulit	shadow puppet theatre using flat leather puppets
wayang kulit purwa	the Javanese shadow puppet theatre

Bibliography

Balfour, Henry L., 'Report on a Collection of Musical Instruments from the Siamese Malay States and Perak', in *Fasciculi Malayanses: Anthropological and Zoological Results of an Expedition to Perak and the Siamese Malay State 1901–2 (Anthropology, Part IIa)*, London: Williams & Norgate for the University of Liverpool Press, 1904.

Becker, A. L., 'Text-building, Epistemology, and Aesthetics in Javanese Shadow Theatre', in A. Yengoyan and A. L. Becker (eds.), *The Imagination of Reality: Essays in Southeast Asian Coherence Systems*, Norwood, NJ: Ablex Publishing Co., 1979.

Becker, Judith, 'The Percussive Patterns in the Music of Mainland Southeast Asia', *Ethnomusicology*, 12, 2 (1968): 173–91.

———, 'Some Thoughts about Pathet, Javanese Modal Classification', Paper read at the International Musicological Society Meeting, Berkeley, California, August 1977.

———, 'Time and Tune in Java', in A. Yengoyan and A. L. Becker (eds.), *The Imagination of Reality: Essays in Southeast Asian Coherence Systems*, Norwood, NJ: Ablex Publishing Co., 1979.

———, 'Toward a Theory of the Derivation of Central Javanese Gamelan Gongan', in *The Traditional Music in Modern Java*, Honolulu: University of Hawaii Press, 1980.

———, *The Traditional Music in Modern Java*, Honolulu: University of Hawaii Press, 1980.

Brunet, Jacques, *Wayang Kulit aus Kelantan*, Berlin: Internationalen Instituts fuer vergleichende Musikstudien und Dokumenation, 1971.

Cole, David, *The Theatrical Event: A Mythos, A Vocabulary, A Perspective*, Middletown, Conn.: Wesleyan University Press, 1975.

Cuisinier, Jeanne, *Danses Magiques de Kelantan*, Paris: Institut D'Ethnologie, 1936.

———, *Le Théâtre d'ombres à Kelantan*, 3rd edn., Paris: Gallimard, 1957.

———, 'The Sacred Books of India and the Malay and Siamese Theatres in Kelantan', *India Arts and Letters*, New Series, VIII, 1 (1934): 43–50.

Dhanit Yupho, *Thai Musical Instruments*, translated from the Thai by David Morton, Bangkok: Department of Fine Arts, 1960.

Eliade, Mircea, *The Myth of the Eternal Return*, Princeton: Princeton University Press, 1954.

———, *The Sacred and the Profane: The Nature of Religion*, translated by Willard R. Trask, New York: Harper, 1959.

———, *Shamanism: Archaic Techniques of Ecstasy*, translated by Willard R. Trask, Princeton: Princeton University Press, 1972.

Endicott, Kirk Michael, *An Analysis of Malay Magic*, Oxford: Clarendon Press, 1970.

Faruqi, Lois Ibsen al, 'Dance as an Expression of Islamic Culture', *Dance Research Journal*, 10, 2 (Spring–Summer 1978): 6–13.

Geertz, Clifford, *The Interpretation of Cultures*, New York: Basic Books, Inc., 1973.

Ghulam-Sarwar Yousof, 'Feasting of the Spirits: The Berjamu Ritual Performance in the Kelantanese *Wayang Siam* Shadow Play', *Kajian Malaysia*, 1, 1 (June 1983): 95–115.

_____, *The Kelantan Mak Yong Dance Theatre: A Study of Performance Structure*, Ann Arbor: University Microfilms, 1976.

_____, *Panggung Semar: Essays on Traditional Malay Theatre*, Kuala Lumpur: Tempo Publications, 1992.

_____, 'The Play of Shadows: Hindu Elements in the Malay *Wayang Kulit Siam*', *India Magazine*, 3, 1 (1982): 32–9.

_____, 'A Previously Unknown Version of the *Ramayana* from Kedah, Malaysia', in D. P. Sinha and Sachchidananda Sahai (eds.), *Ramayana Traditions and National Cultures in Asia*, Lucknow: Directorate of Cultural Affairs and Government of Uttar Pradesh, 1989, pp. 131–7.

_____, 'Ramayana Branch Stories in the *Wayang Siam* Shadow Play of Malaysia', in K. R. Srinivasa Iyengar (ed.), *Asian Variations in Ramayana*, New Delhi: Sahitya Akademi, 1983, pp. 296–323.

Harja Susilo, 'Drumming in the Context of Javanese Gamelan', MA thesis, University of California, Los Angeles, 1967.

Hill, A. H., 'Wayang Kulit Stories from Trengganu', *Journal of the Malayan Branch of the Royal Asiatic Society*, XXII, 3 (June 1949): 85–105.

Hinzler, H. I. R., *Wayang op Bali*, The Hague, 1975.

Hisham Mahzan, 'The Last of the Wayang Kulit Puppeteers', *New Straits Times*, 6 January 1992.

Holt, Claire, *Art in Indonesia: Continuities and Change*, Ithaca, NY: Cornell University Press, 1967.

Humardani, S. D., 'The Wayang Kulit Drama: Its Traditional Stage Performance in Indonesia', in Mohd. Taib Osman (ed.), *Traditional Drama and Music in Southeast Asia*, Kuala Lumpur: Dewan Bahasa dan Pustaka, 1974.

Kennedy, J., *A History of Malaya*, Kuala Lumpur: Macmillan & Co., Ltd., 1964.

Kijang Puteh, 'Talib the Boy Dalang', in *The Straits Times Annual*, 1967, pp. 62–3.

Kirby, Ernest Theodore, *Ur-Drama: The Origins of Theatre*, New York: New York University Press, 1975.

Ku Zam Zam Ku Idris, 'Alat-alat Muzik dalam Ensembel Wayang Kulit, Mek Mulung, dan Gendang Keling di Kedah Utara', in Mohd. Taib Osman and Wan Kadir Yusoff (eds.), *Kajian Budaya dan Masyarakat di Malaysia*, Kuala Lumpur: Dewan Bahasa dan Pustaka, 1983.

Kunst, Jaap, *Hindu–Javanese Musical Instruments*, The Hague: Martinus Nijhoff, 1968.

Lord, Albert B., *The Singer of Tales*, New York: Atheneum, 1973.

Malm, William P., *Music Cultures of the Pacific, the Near East and Asia*, 2nd edn., Englewood Cliffs, NJ: Prentice-Hall, Inc., 1977.

_____, 'Music in Kelantan, Malaysia and Some of Its Cultural Implications', in *Studies in Malaysian Oral and Musical Traditions*, Michigan Papers on South and Southeast Asia, No. 8, Ann Arbor: University of Michigan Press, 1974.

Matusky, Patricia, 'Alat-alat dan Bentuk-bentuk Muzik Tradisi Masyarakat

Melayu', in Mohd. Taib Osman (ed.), *Masyarakat Melayu: Struktur, Organisasi dan Manifestasi*, Kuala Lumpur: Dewan Bahasa dan Pustaka, 1989.

_____, *Music in the Malay Shadow Puppet Theater*, Vols. I–II, Ann Arbor: University Microfilms, 1980.

_____, 'Music of the Mak Yong Theater of Malaysia: A Fusion of Southeast Asian Malay and Middle Eastern Islamic Elements', in Ellen Leichtman (ed.), *To the Four Corners*, Harmonie Park Press, in press.

Mellema, R. L., *Wayang Puppets Carving, Coloring, Symbolism*, translated by Mantle Hood, Amsterdam: Koninklijk Instituut voor de Tropen, 1954.

Mohd. Ghouse Nasaruddin, 'Musik Ethnik Malaysia', in *Bahasa, Kesusasteraan dan Kebudayaan Melayu*, Kuala Lumpur: Kementerian Kebudayaan, Belia dan Sukan Malaysia, 1976.

Mohd. Taib Osman (ed.), *Traditional Drama and Music of Southeast Asia*, Kuala Lumpur: Dewan Bahasa dan Pustaka, 1974.

Morton, David, *The Traditional Instrumental Music of Thailand*, Berkeley: University of California Press, 1976.

Osnes, Mary Beth, 'Malaysia's Evolving Shadow Puppet Theatre', *Asian Theatre Journal*, 9, 1 (Spring 1992): 112–16.

Rahmah Bujang, *Boria: A Form of Malay Theatre*, Singapore: Institute of Southeast Asian Studies, 1987.

_____, 'The Boria: A Study of a Malay Theatre in Its Socio-Cultural Context', Ph.D. thesis, University of Hull, 1977.

Rentse, Anker, 'The Kelantan Shadow-Play (Wayang Kulit)', *Journal of the Malayan Branch of the Royal Asiatic Society*, XIV, 3 (December 1936): 284–301.

Robson, S., *Waŋbaŋ Wideya*, The Hague: Martinus Nijhoff, 1971.

Rutnin, Mattani, 'Nang Yai: The Thai Classical Shadow Play and the Wat Kanon Troupe of Rajburi', *East Asian Cultural Studies*, 15 (March 1976): 53–9.

Sachs, Curt, *The History of Musical Instruments*, New York: W. W. Norton & Co., Inc., 1940.

_____, *The Wellsprings of Music*, edited by Jaap Kunst, New York: McGraw-Hill, 1965.

Scott-Kemball, Jeune, 'The Kelantan *Wayang Siam* Shadow Puppets "Rama" and "Hanuman"', *Man*, 108 (May 1959): 73–8.

Seebas, Tilman, *An Anthology of South-East Asian Music: Panji in Bali I*, Kassel: Baerenreiter-Musicaphon BM 30 SL 2565, Commentary on the recording.

Shahrum bin Yub, 'The Technical Aspects of the Kelantan Malay Shadow Play Theatre', *Federation Museums Journal*, New Series, XV (1970): 43–75.

Sheppard, Dato Haji Mubin, 'Malay Shadow Play Figures in the Museum of Archeology and Ethnology, University of Cambridge', *Federation Museums Journal*, VIII (1963): 14–17.

_____, 'Pa' Dogol and Wa' Long: The Evolution of the Comedians in the Malay Shadow Play in Kelantan', *Journal of the Royal Asiatic Society of Great Britain and Ireland*, XXXVIII, 1 (1965): 1–5.

Simathurai, S., 'Wayang Kulit Goes Modern', *New Straits Times*, 16 March 1992, p. 29.

Skeat, Walter William, *Malay Magic: An Introduction to the Folklore and Popular Religion of the Malay Peninsular*, London: Macmillan & Co., Ltd., 1900; reprinted by Dover, New York, 1967; reissued by Benjamin Blom, New York, 1972.

Skeat, Walter William and Blagden, Charles Otto, *Pagan Races of the Malay Peninsula*, London: Macmillan & Co., Ltd., 1906.

Smithies, Michael, 'The Giant Shadow Play of Thailand', *Orientations*, 4, 8 (August 1973): 47–50.

———, 'Thai Shadow Play Figures', *Arts of Asia*, 3, 5 (September–October 1973): 38–42.

Smithies, Michael and Euayporn Kerdchauay, 'Nang Talung: The Shadow Theatre of Southern Thailand', in Mattani Rutnin (ed.), *The Siamese Theatre: Collection of Reprints from the Journal of the Siam Society*, Bangkok, 1975.

Sweeney, Amin, *Malay Shadow Puppets*, London: The Trustees of the British Museum, 1972.

———, 'The Rama Repertoire in the Kelantan Shadow-Play: A Preliminary Report', *Tenggara*, 5 (1969): 129–33.

———, *The Ramayana and the Malay Shadow Play*, Kuala Lumpur: National University of Malaysia Press, 1972.

Tan Sooi Beng, *Bangsawan: A Social and Stylistic History of Popular Malay Opera*, Singapore: Oxford University Press, 1992.

'Using Wayang Kulit to Woo Voters', *New Straits Times*, 19 December 1991.

Wan Abdul Kadir, *Budaya Popular dalam Masyarakat Melayu Bandaran*, Kuala Lumpur: Dewan Bahasa dan Pustaka, 1988.

Winstedt, Richard, *The Malays: A Cultural History*, rev. edn., Singapore: Graham Brash (Pte) Ltd, 1981.

———, *An Unabridged Malay–English Dictionary*, 6th edn., Kuala Lumpur: Marican & Sons (Malaysia) Sdn. Bhd., 1965.

Index

Numbers in italics refer to Plate numbers.